CONTROL
THE
CONTROLLABLES

CONTROL
THE
CONTROLLABLES

MINDSET, PRESSURE, AND
THE POWER OF CONTROL

RAYMONT
HARRIS

To purchase books in bulk, please contact the publisher.

Mynd Matters Publishing
2690 Cobb Parkway SE, Ste A5-375, Smyrna, GA 30080
www.myndmatterspublishing.com

ISBN: 978-1-963874-68-6 (pbk)
ISBN: 978-1-963874-69-3 (hdcv)
e-ISBN: 978-1-963874-70-9

FIRST EDITION

For those who helped me give language to control.
For the one who helps me live it every day.

THE 8 CONTROLLABLES
A Survival Manual Disguised as a Mindset Framework

This isn't a self-help book. It's not some performance checklist or morning-routine playbook. It's a survival manual built from what I had to learn growing up with weight on my chest, trying to make something of myself before life crushed me first.

The 8 controllables aren't random. They're the tools that saved me. They're how I made it out of Lorain, through Ohio State, into the league, and back again after everything fell apart.

Here's the deal: You can't control outcomes. You can't control people. You can't control timing. But these? You can control. And if you do, they change everything.

- **BELIEF** is where it starts. Not the fake kind. The kind you earn in silence, when nothing's working and you keep showing up anyway.

- **PATIENCE** is what keeps you in it when the dream delays. It's not passive. It's not cute. It's the ability to build when you're invisible.

- **COMMITMENT** is doing the hard shit with no guarantee of recognition. It's showing up when the plan changes, and nobody's checking for you anymore.

- **CONSISTENCY** is what separates the talented from the dangerous. It's doing it right on a Tuesday with no audience and no hype.

- **ADAPTABILITY** is your only option when life doesn't give you time to process. No one's waiting. Either you adjust, or you disappear.

- **EFFORT** is more than working hard. It's doing the right hard work. The kind that takes intention, not just sweat.

- **POSITIVITY** isn't hype or fake smiles. It's a decision to stay open and useful even when you're hurting.

- **RESILIENCE** is what you build when it all goes off-script. It's recovering in real time—while still carrying your people and your purpose.

Control the Controllables walks through all eight. Each one has its own chapter, built from real stories, hard moments, and no polish. Every chapter ends with a simple breakdown: a Playbook you can actually use. Not theory. Not inspiration. Just weapons for real life.

I didn't write this to impress anyone. I wrote it because I know what it's like to feel like everything's out of your hands. This is how you get your power back.

If you've ever felt like your life doesn't have a backup plan, this is for you.

It's for those carrying more than they can say but still showing up. For the athletes, the underdogs, and the leaders under pressure. For anybody tired of hearing "just be positive" while fighting to stay above water. For anyone who's ever asked, "What can I actually control right now?"

Welcome to *Control the Controllables*.

CONTENTS

Introduction: *Why I Wrote This*   *13*

Chapter **1:** BELIEF
        The Foundation That Changes Everything.................. 17

Chapter **2:** PATIENCE
        The Wait That Builds You 41

Chapter **3:** COMMITMENT
        The Line Between Interest and Investment 63

Chapter **4:** POSITIVITY
        Hard-Earned 85

Chapter **5:** ADAPTABILITY
        Who You Were Won't Be Enough 107

Chapter **6:** CONSISTENCY
        Where the Real Ones Separate 125

Chapter **7:** RESILIENCE
        Built Through the Hits 145

Chapter **8:** EFFORT
        Paid in Full 167

Chapter **9:** ELITE MINDSET & PERFORMANCE
        Built from Every Controllable 189

Chapter **10:** THE COMBO MANUAL
        Making EMP Work in Real Life 209

Special Acknowledgments   *219*

WHY I WROTE THIS

It always seems to happen around midnight. My son calls it 'Demon Time'. When the house is quiet. When the front you wear all day finally drops, that's when people call me.

Last time, it was a kid on scholarship, super talented, star recruit. But not anymore. He'd lost his spot. His whole world was collapsing in on itself so fast he couldn't breathe. The fear was coming in waves. His voice cracked on the phone like he didn't recognize it.

He said, "I don't know who I am anymore."

And that hit me. Because I know EXACTLY what that feels like.

I grew up in Lorain, Ohio. Back when steel ran the city. Back when survival was the win. I didn't grow up with inspirational quotes on the walls. I grew up watching my father grind to keep our family together after we lost our mom. I watched the way people in my neighborhood were beaten down but kept showing up. And without even realizing it, I started building a system in my head. I started grabbing on to anything I could control, the one thing nobody could take from me: how I responded when life pushed.

That mindset got me to THE Ohio State University. Then to the NFL. It worked, until it didn't.

When the league ended, I lost everything I'd built my identity around. I remember lying on the floor in my boy's basement after my separation, no marriage, no purpose, just disappointment ringing through my head like a siren. Failure screams. And that shit was loud as hell.

That's when it hit.

All the things I leaned on when I was coming up, the effort, the resilience, the belief, the way I learned to adapt and reset, I still had those. I just hadn't been using them. I'd gotten so used to the world handing me structure that I forgot how to build it for myself.

I forced myself to start building again.

I kept leaning on the same things that helped me survive Lorain, that raw grit that teaches you to survive harder. The stuff that held together when everything else broke. That's how EMP started. Quietly. Just me, figuring out how to rebuild with what was already in my hands.

EMP is the system I created from what saved me. From what actually worked when life broke me down.

These eight controllables form a complete system that naturally breaks down into two main categories:

MINDSET Controls (B.P.C.P.)

- **BELIEF**: Your foundation that something better is possible
- **POSITIVITY**: Your ability to spot opportunities when everyone else sees problems
- **COMMITMENT**: Your dedication to keep going when it's no longer convenient
- **PATIENCE**: Your understanding of how time and process actually work

PERFORMANCE Controls (C.A.R.E.)

- **CONSISTENCY**: Your ability to show up and deliver, regardless of how you feel
- **ADAPTABILITY**: Your skill at adjusting when life changes (and it always changes)
- **RESILIENCE**: Your power to bounce back stronger after getting knocked down
- **EFFORT**: Your energy focused on stuff that actually matters

When these pieces come together, they create something that holds no matter what hits you. The kind of strength that lasts because you built it yourself.

We're not talking about hacks or viral motivation. It's about control. Controlling you. The only true control you'll ever have.

This is exactly what I live by. Real talk, this is the mindset that saved me. And this right here is what I'm passing on now. I've watched it work with everyone from pro athletes and C-Suite decision makers to young brothers trying to find themselves after the spotlight moves on.

This system gave them something to hold. A way through. And I'm telling you right now, it can do the same for you.

So don't read this like a manual. Don't try to memorize it. Just sit with it. Let it call you out. Let it remind you of what you've always had.

That athlete who texted me at midnight? By morning, he had a plan, not just for sports, but for life.

This book isn't built for the highlight reel. It's for the storm, for the moment when your identity starts slipping and you need something solid to hold.

Controlling the controllables keeps you solid when life tries to break you.

You're carrying too much that doesn't belong to you, but you're not broken, and you're damn sure not done.

Let's lighten the load.

Let's rebuild the system.

Let's get to work.

CHAPTER 1

BELIEF: THE FOUNDATION THAT CHANGES EVERYTHING

BELIEF is the first cornerstone of our **MINDSET** controls. Without it, none of the others stand for long.

Lorain, Ohio. Friday night lights cutting through the haze from the steel mill. I'm standing on the sidelines, anxious, heart pounding so hard my shoulder pads were shaking. Junior year at Admiral King High School. Third-string running back. Invisible to everyone... except Mr. Herrmann.

My geometry teacher. Offensive line coach. One of the few who could see past the tough guy act I wore like armor.

Lorain ain't a place that hands out dreams for free. Steel town where hope rusts faster than the auto plants, but the people are cut from steel.

My Pops worked that mill and the auto plants for more than 40 years. He raised me and my siblings on his own after my mom died just four days after I was born.

I never got to know her. But the space she left behind never went away. Sometimes I'd catch my Pops staring through me, like just seeing me reminded him of everything he'd lost.

I can't imagine what that type of loss does to a man, especially a Black man from a generation where therapy was for 'crazy people'.

His love didn't feel like love. It felt like anger and judgment in disguise.

Everything I did was wrong. Or never quite enough.

Sometimes, if I had a good game, he'd leave the newspaper out where I could see it. No speech. No pat on the back. Just the paper on the kitchen table or stuck to the fridge like, "You did alright."

That was as close to proud as I would see.

It took me years to understand what I was really seeing. A man fighting battles he didn't have the words to explain.

That's the thing about that "old-school Black man from the South love," it comes wrapped in thorns. Every lukewarm "that was ok" is buried under three critiques and a backhanded compliment about somebody else.

Some of us still pass that down without even thinking. "I'm not gonna tell them they did a good job, gotta keep 'em hungry." Maybe it keeps them hungry. But it also keeps them doubting.

My question: Is that lesson worth raising someone full of self-doubt...who grows up resenting you?

I remember pushing that busted Chevette up and down the driveway at six in the morning, breath turning into clouds in the cold. It may have been freezing, but there was a burn inside me that wouldn't let me stop. I knew my boys weren't doing this crazy shit, this was the work that would separate me. They had talent...I had something else.

That Friday night, our star running back goes down. Then his backup drops too. The stadium got so quiet you could hear the trucks rumbling next to George Daniel Field.

I wasn't happy those dudes got hurt. But that's the game.

Coach Herrmann caught my eye. And right there, his words from the week before felt heavier: "Ray, most of these folks just see a backup. Life is about timing. When your time comes, show them what I see... I see a starter waiting for his shot. Question is, what do you see?"

My mouth was dry as hell. Excitement. Fear. Everything I built in the dark was stepping into the light.

No more hiding.
No more waiting.
Ball snaps.
The world slows.
It feels like the Matrix.

I can hear every "you ain't ready" echo in my head.

My number gets called. Hand off up the middle. Shake a tackler. Run through another.

Seventy yards later, I'm standing in the end zone.

The crowd's roaring, but I barely hear it. I'm hearing my Pops: "I thought you were fast. You should've gone to the left."

But this time, my voice was louder than his.

As my teammates swarmed me, I felt the breakthrough.

Something deeper than pride or validation.

The doubts were still there, they just moved to the backseat.

Standing there, surrounded by noise I couldn't even process, I realized the work had already proved itself. And so had I.

That night on the field changed what I knew.

It's easy to mistake belief for hype or blind confidence. Proof-based belief is earned. It's built through the work that nobody sees.

Here's the difference: If your belief is built off outside praise or somebody else's approval, it disappears the second things get hard. But if it's built off your own proof, it sticks. Even when everything around you is shaky.

This is the line most never cross. They wait. For the coach to call their number. For the boss to validate their effort. For someone else to tell them they're enough before they decide to believe it themselves.

Put your belief in someone else's hands, and you give away the whole damn game.

What clicked for me that night wasn't, "I'm worthy because I scored." It was, "I'd been worthy the whole time." The touchdown just made it obvious to everybody else.

Once you've built it that way? It carries everything else you do.

Every lonely stadium stair. Every tire flip or sled push.

Unconventional work brought unconventional success.

Just know...belief is built in the dark.

Understanding Belief

That night changed me. Friday night lights. The whole city was watching. It showed me what belief really is, and what it isn't.

Growing up in Lorain, I learned there are three levels of belief. Most people get stuck at the first. Some push into the second. But that third one changes everything.

Surface Belief: Looks the Part

This is the belief that only works when things are going your way.

I saw it at Admiral King, guys with crazy talent but never built the foundation or the armor underneath. Belief was easy when things looked good. But the second adversity hit? They vanished, talked tough, but moved soft.

Their belief was built on recognition, not repetition. On what people saw, not what they didn't.

Surface belief can carry you through a good game. Maybe a season. But it won't survive a career. The long game demands more. And it always collects.

Validation Belief: Fueled by Doubt

This one runs deeper, and it burns hotter.

These are the grinders. In the gym before school. On the field after practice. Working hard because they've got something to prove.

I lived in this space for years, out there before dawn, lungs on fire, moving anything heavy I could find. Attacking those park bench workouts long after everyone else had gone home.

That voice in my head kept pushing me to prove the doubters wrong.

Especially my Pops.

He never said he was proud, but I trained like he might.

After every accomplishment, I thought the same thing: maybe this is the one that breaks through.

That voice in my head pushed me harder than any coach ever could. I waited for it to shut up. It never did.

You think you're building yourself, but you're really just trying to get picked.

When your belief depends on proving people wrong, they're still running the show. They still own your grind.

And when the cheering stops? So does your momentum.

Validation belief feels strong because it pushes you, but it never feeds you. You can't build anything solid when you're starving for someone else's recognition.

I didn't know it yet, but their thoughts were never the point. It had to come from me. Not a performance. Not a reaction. My choice.

That was the turn.

Not because I felt strong. But because I finally stopped chasing the doubters and started listening to my own voice.

Transformative Belief: This Is Mine Now

Transformative belief becomes part of your identity. It's not something you need to prove anymore, it's just who you are.

Not for the scoreboard. Not for the spotlight. It's who you are when no one's asking.

It shows up during the in-between. When you're buried on the depth chart but still going. When the reps feel thankless, but you take them anyway. You stop waiting. You just become.

In that moment, doubt stopped running the show.

No pep talk. No fake hype. The proof was already there. The foundation already built. Mr. Herrmann modeled that same steadiness. In how he carried himself. In how he treated me. Sometimes it takes someone else's belief to remind you of your own. Solid. Unshaken.

Belief isn't a feeling. It's not confidence. It's the proof you've already built. It's the quiet certainty from putting in work when everyone's gone home. From staying ready even when your chance seems distant.

Because every rep builds something permanent. Something no result, or setback, can ever undo.

Importance of Belief

Belief becomes your lifeline when everything else slips. It shapes how you show up, physically, mentally, and emotionally.

And when the world starts pressing, it's the only thing that can't be borrowed.

Physical Challenges: Earned in the Dark

When demons come to negotiate in those quiet hours, they whisper convincing arguments: "Nobody's watching. Why push today...do it tomorrow?"

And they're right, nobody would've known if I'd stayed in bed. But those solo workouts answered the real question:

Are you built for this, or just acting like it?

Every moment in the cold became a choice between comfort and growth, between what was easy and what was necessary.

When it's just you, the wind, and nothing but your own will pushing forward, no fans, no validation, you learn what your belief is really built on

These physical tests force you to prove whether what you want is worth what it costs.

These challenges reveal the truth. Do you just talk belief, or do you live it?

Mental Challenges: You vs. You

Being third string humbles the hell out of you.

I'd walk home from practice with my cleats over my shoulder, fighting back tears, watching starters run plays while a voice in my head kept saying: "Maybe they're right. Maybe you're not good enough."

The worst part? Sometimes that voice sounded like my Pops.

Not because he said those exact words, but because his silence left too much space for doubt to speak.

You can't outrun that voice when it's inside you.

Mental battles cut deeper than physical ones. Even when your body's ready, belief is what decides if you show up like you belong.

There were days I didn't think I'd ever start. Some days I thought this might be it. But I kept showing up, angry, unsure, and that became the proof.

Confidence alone won't carry you. You need proof, proof that you can still choose yourself when no one else does.

Belief is steady. It shows up when you don't feel strong. And it keeps you from quitting when nobody would blame you if you did.

Family Challenges: The Words He Never Said

My father lost his wife when I entered this world. Every time he looked at me, he saw both his greatest love and his deepest loss. That kind of pain built a wall I could never break through, no matter what I did.

My mother died giving birth to me. That sentence carries more weight than I've ever been able to explain. I never got to meet her. Never got to hear her voice, her presence, her softness or her protection. But somehow, I carried her loss like it was mine to answer for.

I grew up in a house built on sacrifice. My Pops did everything he could to hold it together. But the grief sat between us, heavy and unspoken. It shaped everything through the tension between us. Those long silences carried a weight I couldn't escape just by being his son.

I spent years pushing beyond limits just to hear that man say, "I'm proud of you." Partly for attention, but really to feel like I belonged in this story that started with so much pain. What I needed to hear and what I got were never the same. But the hunger stayed, and that kept me alive longer than comfort would have.

He never said it. But the growth came when I stopped chasing it, when I accepted that some belief just has to grow in the mud.

I inherited more than just his silence. The grief he carried became mine too, even when neither of us could name it.

Family plants the first seeds of belief or doubt. Growing up with those expectations, that history, those unspoken rules, it changes how you build confidence.

The belief that survives family pressure develops muscles that can handle whatever comes next. Because the world's judgment rarely hits as hard as what you already faced at home.

Family pressure carries a heavier weight. You're fighting everything expected, and everything unsaid. If you can build belief carrying all that, nothing else will ever be too heavy.

Social Challenges: Bigger Than the Block

In Lorain, dreaming big felt like betrayal. Say you wanted to play D1, and somebody older would smirk, like you'd just said something disrespectful. Like you broke some unspoken code: don't dream bigger than where you're from.

I hadn't started a single game yet. I was still buried on the depth chart, no tape, no stats, nothing to prove I belonged. And still, I said it out loud: 'I'm gonna play Division I football.'

Some laughed, some pulled back. It wasn't just doubt. It was distance. Belief makes people uncomfortable when they've already given up on theirs.

The block had seen too many dreamers fall. Friends side-eyed the extra workouts. Family didn't know the path. And deep down, nobody wanted to be the one left behind.

Your ambition starts to sound like disrespect. Like you think you're better. Like you forgot where you're from.

When Dennis Washington signed with Michigan, he didn't just get a scholarship. He gave me permission.

Proof that it wasn't betrayal to believe, it was survival.

Belief like that costs you. People pull back. The room gets quiet.

But in the silence, belief either holds, or it folds.

You stop waiting to be understood. You stop needing their permission. You just build.

And when you do, your dream doesn't shrink to fit your world. Your world expands to fit your dream.

Cultivating Belief

Belief Without a Blueprint

I had belief, but no instructions. No older cousin to call, no map to follow. Just instincts, trial and error, and a vision I couldn't shake.

Athletes were everywhere in my family. It was in the bloodline. My dad's oldest brother Isaiah Harris was an All-Star pitcher for the Memphis Red Sox in the Negro Leagues. He and his brothers were all ball players too. When they moved north to Lorain, they traded their ball caps for hard hats, steel mill jobs paid better than chasing their dreams. My Pops had the chance to follow his brother to the league, but he chose the mill instead. He still carved out his own name, becoming a legend in local softball leagues.

My cousins were city legends. James "Bubbles" Harris. Tommie "Hollywood" Harris. My cousins ran Lorain basketball. My older brother Rennie followed in their steps. Baseball and basketball. That was the standard in my family.

But football? Nobody had taken that road. Not to college and damn sure not the League.

Once I started chasing that path, I was proud of where I came from, but I also felt alone as hell.

I wasn't trying to mimic anyone. I was trying to figure out what success even looked like for someone like me.

That made it heavier. I was chasing something new while carrying the pressure of everything my family had already done. I'd walk through the city and hear people say, "That's Rennie's little brother." Or "That's one of them Harris boys." And I was, but I also wasn't. I was building something of my own.

I remember lying awake some nights, just trying to picture what it would feel like to walk onto a college field and belong. I didn't know what it looked like. I just knew I wanted to get there.

Belief without a blueprint feels like walking blind, step by step, hoping the ground holds. Trying to carry your roots into something none of them could show you.

I had to figure it out step by step. No guarantee. Just laying one stone at a time, hoping the path I built would be strong enough to carry me forward."

Let That Hurt Work

Belief often needs to see itself in someone else first. The first time you see someone pull off what felt impossible, it changes everything. At Hawthorne Boone Junior High, Dennis Washington owned those hallways in his orange #20 jersey, commanding respect wherever he walked. He proved you didn't have to leave Lorain to become somebody. Standing in line for jerseys, I asked for #20, so I could be like D-Wash. Coach laughed, "You'll never be as good as Dennis." I've never forgotten that. Maybe you've had your own version, getting written off before you even got a shot.

I'd like to say I brushed it off and was the bigger man, but I didn't. I was 14, angry, and embarrassed. I didn't talk to anyone, because I didn't know how. I just held onto it like I held onto every other slight or doubt I'd ever heard. I carried that line with me like a scar, quiet, but always there.

Back then, I trained to prove people wrong. To build something in myself they'd have to respect whether they liked me or not. And deep down, I wanted my Pops to see it too. To finally look at me and say, "I'm proud of you." I knew it probably wouldn't happen, but I chased it anyway. That chase became part of the fire that kept me burning longer than it should've.

The crazy part? It worked. That pain turned into fuel. But I've often wondered: Could belief even fix what was built from something broken?

I Saw It Before They Did

Before you ever get your name called, belief has to show up like it already belongs.

When I was third-string at Admiral King High, the coaches didn't see me on the field, so I had to. I'd visualize the cuts, the runs, the crowd noise, the celebration in the end zone. Every detail had to feel real, because they were building something I'd need later.

Before games, I'd close my eyes and run the plays full speed in my head. I'd feel defenders bounce off my big ass shoulder pads. When the opportunity came against Sandusky, my mind had already been there. The game felt slower because I was ready.

It sounds like something mystical, but it's actually just mental training, getting the work in when I couldn't do it physically. And yeah, the science backs it up. The brain doesn't know the difference between a full-speed rep in your head and a real one on the field. That mental work matters. It wires your belief before the world ever gives you the stage.

Visualization gave me that familiarity. It felt like I'd already been there, like I was stepping into something I already owned.

Mr. Herrmann got it before I ever did. "When your time comes," he said, "show them all what I see."

That stuck with me. He believed for me until I could see it. Clear enough that when my time came, it felt familiar. But belief doesn't just grow. It gets hit. And if you're not ready for that, it won't last.

Overcoming Challenges to Belief

They Stopped Calling My Name

Senior year, I was ready. Best shape of my life. The offense ran through me. Every practice felt like proof I was about to take off. And then one hit took it all. It was a meaningless scrimmage and somebody cheap-shotted me in the pile after the whistle. I got angry, pushed back, tried to kick him off. That's when my knee strained and I heard the pop. I'd lost my cool and paid for it. First three games, gone. I zoned in on rehab like my life depended on it.

And then, crack. My collarbone.

The noise landed before the pain and the room went quiet because I already knew the score. The doctor barely looked up when he said, "Season's over." I didn't argue. I went home and cried. I had fought my way back after the knee and scraped through three and a half games. Then this. That second hit didn't just stop a season. It crushed the version of belief I thought I had. What stayed behind was something heavier and more honest. It was me standing in a broken season with nothing left to prove, choosing to keep showing up.

When Your Hero Becomes Your Mirror

Junior year. We're playing our rivals, Lorain High. The buzz around that game was real because of one name: Dennis Washington. He was the top running back in the district by far. His game was nice. He had speed, balance, smooth footwork, grown-man swag. He was the man. Even though he was one year older, I looked up to him.

In some fantasy version of this story, I'd be the underdog who gets his first shot against his idol and becomes a legend. Well, Lorain ain't Hollywood and this wasn't the Hallmark Channel.

I stood on the sideline in a clean uniform and watched Dennis run through our defense like we weren't even there. This was his showcase. And I felt tiny and embarrassed. Like I wasn't even there. My idol was writing another chapter of his legacy, and I was just standing on the sidelines reading the story. I wasn't even a footnote in his highlight reel. That stuck with me. I kept replaying it, watching how I disappeared while he wrote the story.

It made me question whether I belonged in the book at all.

That night messed with me. I didn't have the words for it back then, but my foundation was shook. The belief I'd been building all year took a hit as I watched what greatness looked like, and I didn't feel anywhere close to it.

Fast forward one year to senior season.

Dennis was off to college. I missed the first three games with an injury, but I made it back just in time to play Lorain High. We blew their doors off. I rushed for over 300 yards and scored five touchdowns. That night people learned my name. That was my redemption.

Years later, after OSU, I got invited back to speak at my old junior high. Walking those halls, everything looked smaller. Trophies in the case. Photos on the wall. Then I saw it: the orange #20 jersey was the only jersey...retired.

I assumed it was D-Wash's.

But it wasn't. It was retired for me.

That day didn't feel like a victory, it felt like a reckoning. And I finally understood what belief had been building in me the whole time.

That walk through my old junior high? It showed me belief carries memory and weight, becoming something that once felt out of reach.

That moment hit me hard. Not as a flex, but as a full-circle check-in. I'd spent so long trying to be worthy in the eyes of my hero that I didn't realize I'd become what I once admired. And the wildest part? it happened by just being me and not trying to be him.

It came back during those early mornings when my legs were still heavy from the day before, and I showed up anyway. No magic. Just steady proof.

And when it finally clicks, you realize you don't need to chase someone else's greatness. You just needed to run to your own.

That Version of Me Didn't Survive

That night after the collarbone break, everything got quieter. No calls on the landline. No teammates stopping by. No reporters at the door. Just me and the walls. And the sound of a dream cracking under its own weight.

When the first injury happened, I had something to fight for, getting back in time to save my senior year.

When the second one happened, there was no season left to save. Belief had to find a new form.

My motivation completely changed. The scoreboard, the depth chart, even making doubters eat their words didn't drive me anymore. A different beast had taken over.

It came down to one thing: Can you still move forward when the outcome you wanted is gone?

I had to find a way to keep showing up when there was no finish line left in sight. No spotlight waiting. No payoff coming.

I started small. Show up for rehab even when nobody's watching your progress. Push through those exercises when nothing seems to matter anymore. The season might be over, but the work never stops, because you're building something beyond the scoreboard.

This belief wasn't flashy. Just that quiet burn that keeps showing up when everything else tries to pull you away.

The kind you carry when everyone else moves on. The kind that says: even if the dream bends, I don't break with it.

The true test is whether you can believe enough to rebuild when everything falls apart.

The scoreboard was dark. But I kept showing up. Because belief doesn't stop when the lights go out.

Success Story: Tyler Perry

I've talked about belief through sports and family dynamics, plus the doubt that shapes it all. But some stories stretch way beyond the field and still carry that same weight.

You want to see what belief looks like in the flesh? Not Tyler Perry the billionaire, but the man sleeping in his Geo Metro between shifts, writing plays on yellow legal pads while his family called him crazy.

His stories came from real pain. His father's beatings were so severe that he once blacked out for three days. That same trauma that drove him to contemplate suicide became fuel for his first play, "I Know I've Been Changed."

Perry invested his entire savings, $12,000 from working whatever jobs would hire him, into that first production. It flopped spectacularly: 30 people in a 1,200-seat theater.

Most people would've called it. But Perry looked at that empty theater and said, "I'm not done yet." For six years, SIX YEARS, he lived out of his car, rewrote that play 15 times, and staged it wherever possible. No safety net. No Plan B. Just him, his story, and absolute belief.

"I was running from poverty, from abuse, from a father who I felt didn't love me," Perry says. But here's the difference: He kept going, even when he didn't know where it would lead. Belief doesn't erase the pain. It just gives you a reason to keep walking through it.

In 1998, he gave it one more try after six years of nothing but failure. This time? The show sells out. Not for one night, for a week. Then tours nationally. That same play that flopped runs for eight straight years.

Most would have settled for a successful theater career. Not Perry. He didn't ask for a seat at Hollywood's table, he built his own. His 330-acre studio complex in Atlanta stands larger than Warner Bros, Disney, and Paramount combined.

The part that gives me chills: He built it on former Confederate Army grounds. A Black man who grew up in poverty, building an empire on land that once denied his humanity. That wasn't just a win. That was belief taking back the ground it was never supposed to touch.

Perry's story hits me because I see parallels to my own journey, different paths, same core truth. Whether you're a kid from Lorain pushing a Chevette at dawn or a man sleeping in his Geo Metro between auditions, there's always that moment where you're told to quit. Some just don't listen.

Belief Conclusion: What I Built Couldn't Be Broken

I didn't get here because someone handed me a plan. Or showed me how to believe. I got here by building it when nobody else could see it.

What I had at first barely looked like belief. But it was mine. And I kept it alive while everything else tried to bury it.

Between the weight I inherited and the doubts I created, belief had to fight for space.

I trained like it mattered before anybody cared. Unconventional workouts. Visualizing plays I hadn't even lived yet. Held onto scars and turned them into fuel. Wanted to be seen by my Pops so badly it hurt. And kept chasing it anyway, even when it didn't come.

I couldn't see the finish line. But I knew I wasn't the same kid who started the race.

Belief is the choice to keep moving when everything else says stop. Becoming someone who keeps moving forward even when the map runs out. It means you stay in it until there's no way to ignore you. However long it takes.

If belief is the thing that carried you this far, here's how to carry it on purpose.

EMPowered to Act: Your Belief Blueprint

Prove It to Yourself First - Belief gets built in silence. Every early morning workout. Every time you showed up without recognition. Pick something small and keep doing it. Let your consistency speak louder than your doubts.

Build It Without A Map - Nobody in my family played D1 football. I wasn't sure the path, I just started walking. Sometimes the plan is not clear. You need belief that survives the uncertainty. What's one move you can make today even if the outcome isn't clear yet?

Visualize Before It's Real - At Admiral King, I was third-string. I didn't get reps, so I made them in my head. Those mental reps stick. Your body remembers what your mind already ran. Take five minutes today and see it before it happens. Let your mind train what your hands haven't touched yet.

Remember: Belief without action is just wishful thinking. The only permission you need is your own. Never forget the core truth, belief is 100% in your control.

So now what? If belief's on you, then this is where you start.

CHAPTER 2

PATIENCE: THE WAIT THAT BUILDS YOU

PATIENCE is the second cornerstone of our **MINDSET** controls. It's what belief leans on when life drags its feet. When you've done the work, earned the shot, but the results won't show up. It's a power move. Patience is the art of staying in it when everything inside you is screaming to quit.

But here's what I learned the hard way: Belief don't mean much if it crumbles the minute results get slow. You can trust yourself, but if you can't sit in that trust while the clock drags, it'll collapse on you. Patience is what keeps belief from turning into doubt.

When I replay it now, I see what patience actually requires. We've been taught it's just waiting, just holding on until your shot comes. But that mindset kills growth.

At its core, patience demands you to build while you wait and use the time to become the kind of person who's ready for your chance when it happens.

Here's where the average person goes wrong. They treat patience like punishment. Like something they just have to survive until life gets fair. Every day someone else gets the spotlight feels like a day stolen from them. That thinking eats away at your energy. You spend your time stewing instead of grinding.

You have to decide: is it a delay, or the development you need? Are you clocking time or putting in work? One mindset leaves you bitter. The other makes you undeniable.

The trap is thinking patience means doing nothing. That if you wait long enough, your turn shows up. But time alone doesn't hand out rewards. The real reward is what you turn into while nobody's watching."

Back then, all I knew was this: I'd been grinding for a year with nothing guaranteed, and something finally felt like it was clicking.

Spring 1990. Ohio State practice field. Sun beating down. Jersey stuck to sweaty shoulder pads. Legs shot, lungs on fire. But I was still standing. Still up. Still there. That kind of earned exhaustion tells you something: I belonged.

After a year of getting my ass kicked on the scout team, I'd finally made it, first-string running back heading into Year Two. Coaches would give me that nod like, "Alright." Teammates showing love. I could feel it. I was in the mix now.

It felt damn good. But the moment it feels like you made it is usually when things start to slip.

Three months later, first day of Camp, I saw the future walk through the door. Robert Smith. Gatorade Player of the Year.

Two-time Ohio Mr. Football. Long strides and effortless. He didn't have to say a word to change the air in the room.

I knew who he was. We all did.

At first, I wasn't impressed. Smooth, yeah. Fast, no doubt. But I'd seen fast before. It wasn't until the actual games that I really saw it: he erased angles and beat defenders to the corner every damn time. I knew then, this guy was legit.

And just like that, my name dropped without anyone saying a word.

I thought I was next. I'd put in the work, climbed the depth chart, felt like I'd finally earned it. Then Robert walked in and the room leaned his way. I went from rising to replaced. I hadn't taken a wrong step, but the room had already moved on. What his arrival really did was hit my confidence. I thought I had a foundation, then I realized how shaky it still was."

And that voice came back, the one that knows exactly how to push your buttons. "You did all that work for this? You're a backup again. Transfer. Go somewhere you're wanted." That voice doesn't yell. It whispers and it's logical. Like it's protecting you.

I gave him the nickname, "Juice." Because of the #32 and the OJ Simpson style with long strides. It was me making peace with the new reality without making it personal. Giving him his respect without giving up my own lane.

Juice was smooth and effortless. I was power and dirty work. We weren't the same, but we were on the same field. That was enough to keep me in the fight, not against him but for myself. I was still the same guy in the same room. The difference now was how I carried it."

That whole season was a masterclass in patience. Waiting without pouting. Working without guarantees. And putting up numbers when your number was called. Patience is standing in the unknown without letting it own you.

Understanding Patience

Patience meant one thing in Lorain, and something completely different in Columbus.

Back home, it meant pushing through. In Columbus, it meant something harder, standing tall while watching other guys live your dream.

In Lorain, I knew every street and rhythm. At Ohio State, I walked into a city 13 times the size of mine, where the student population nearly matched my entire hometown.

Everywhere I looked: new faces, new energy, new expectations. Guys from Florida, Georgia, Texas, California, each one the man in his hometown. Just like me.

Then the ankle rolled, the redshirt came, and I landed on the scout team. That's when patience stopped being a word and became survival.

And over time, I realized it moves through levels. Most people never get past the first.

Surface Patience: Just Waiting

This is what most people mistake for patience, enduring until things change.

I saw it every day on the scout team. Guys going through the motions. Complaining in drills. Counting down days like they were doing time.

There was one five-star recruit who literally checked off practices on a calendar. He'd mutter, "Just gotta make it through." His body was there, but mentally? He was gone.

He thought patience was just waiting. What he never saw was that the waiting WAS the test.

By the time opportunity knocked, he wasn't ready. He'd spent a whole year waiting instead of building.

Eventually, he transferred out, but nothing changed. New squad. Same mindset. Still waiting on the dream to show up, instead of preparing to meet it.

Surface patience looks like holding on, but all you're really doing is wasting time.

Strategic Patience: The Wait Was Work

The next level of patience does more than wait. It builds.

After the redshirt and the move to scout team I had one choice: check out or show up. I showed up. I treated every rep like it counted. I watched the guys I wanted to be: Anthony Thompson, Darrell Thompson, Leroy Hoard. I watched tape, took notes, then tested what I learned against the starters.

On scout team they tried to take my head off every snap. They saw a crash test dummy. I flipped it. I started delivering the collisions and doing the driving.

That redshirt year became my proving ground. During bowl practice I was running with the first string when a blitz I'd seen a hundred times on scout showed up. I saw the hole before the snap, stoned the safety and put him on his back. I ran back for high fives and a wink from Coach T. That pass protection turned heads because it came from getting my ass kicked in practice, again and again.

It wasn't luck. Scout team reps paid off. Off the field, when professors looked at me like I didn't belong, I didn't argue. I made Academic All-Big Ten and let the grades speak. When folks back home didn't get my new world, I leaned on teammates who were living it with me.

Strategic patience was where I did the work. The waiting became the proving ground.

Transformative Patience: Wasn't My Script

The deepest level showed up when Robert Smith arrived.

I had just fought through the scout team. Climbed the depth chart. It felt like it was finally my turn.

Then the nation's top recruit walks in.

Part of me wanted to hate him. But during a scrimmage, after he broke a long run, I marveled like everyone else. And that actually threw me off.

Wasn't he taking my carries? Why was I rooting for him?

Something clicked into place, clearer than it had ever been.

His success didn't steal from mine. We weren't canceling each other out, we were making each other better

Juice and I were different, he was smooth, and made guys miss. I was grimy and ran through dudes. But that difference? It made us both better. And it made the team stronger.

I chose to let patience change me.

It stopped being about waiting your turn and started becoming trust in your growth.

Scout team wasn't part of the dream. Splitting carries wasn't what I pictured.

But both made me better, if I let them.

Some guys count the days. Some grind through them. But the ones who transform? They make the wait do something to them.

I watched it play out over and over at school. The guys who just endured usually transferred or quit. The ones who worked during the wait became solid players. But those few who actually let the experience change them? They usually became something better than they ever thought.

The waits are where you get made. Show up for them.

Importance of Patience

Patience goes deeper than character. It's a performance skill.

It decides how you handle injuries, depth charts, silence, systems, and people who don't see your full value, yet.

The ones who master it? They grow deeper. Because when everything else speeds up, patience is how you stay in control.

Physical Challenges: Down. Not Done.

Day one at Ohio State smacked me in the mouth. The weight room was full of grown-ass men, years into real strength programs. I thought I was strong. I was average.

Then I rolled my ankle in camp. Just like that, the plays I'd been visualizing and the reps I'd been waiting on were gone. Instead of breaking out I was in ankle circles and toe raises. Training room purgatory.

Mentally I was ready. Physically, I was benched. The body does not care how bad you want it. Rush it and it breaks. The redshirt felt like punishment and it messed with my head more than the injury did.

The scout team became my physical lab. I took hits from dudes headed to the NFL. Some guys folded under the lumps and the silence. I treated every rep like it mattered. Same bruises. Different outcome.

Mental Challenges: Mind Playing Tricks On Me

The mental part is quieter, but it cuts deeper.

That voice in your head turns up when you're on the sideline and everyone else is shining. You start to feel invisible, like you're fading. Calls from home slow down, people ask what's wrong, and the doubt grabs hold: maybe you missed your shot, maybe they were right.

The worst moments were the quiet ones, me alone in the dorm on a Saturday, watching the team get ready and wondering if my turn would ever come.

I couldn't shut the thoughts off, and pretending did nothing. What worked was a different move: let the doubt hang there, but don't hand it the controls. I stopped seeing Juice, Butler, and Carlos as obstacles and started studying them. I watched how they moved. I copied what worked. I did the small things every day. When I stopped fighting the delay, the delay started working for me.

Relationship Challenges: Connection Came Second

Columbus dropped me into a different world. Teammates came from places I didn't know. Coaches moved like every day was life or death. A campus that swallowed you if you let it. At first, I took it personal. If it didn't click, I thought it meant I didn't belong.

Then I realized we weren't enemies. Robert ran like he belonged and the room answered him. Coaches were doing their job, not scheming against me. The campus wasn't cold. It was unfamiliar. As a Black kid from Lorain, a lot of people already had me filed under "football." I had to pick my battles and decide when to stand and when to keep it moving. Patience meant showing up and letting them see it. Connection came later. I built it by being steady.

Career Challenges: This Ain't Linear

Football doesn't give you decades. You get a couple seasons to prove everything. And that pressure? It makes people desperate.

I saw it all the time, players transferring too soon or blowing up on coaches. Some refused to change roles that could've extended their career. Impatience wrecked more dudes than injury ever did.

My path didn't look anything like I pictured. From redshirt to backup, then starting to sharing time. Eventually they moved me from tailback to fullback. That was never the script I had in mind

But I got surgical with what I could control instead of chasing the perfect opportunity. I trained different and showed up different. Let go of trying to predict anything.

I watched guys blow up their careers trying to force a moment. Trying to speed up timing that wasn't theirs yet. I learned to let go of the noise and just work.

And that change of mindset did so much for my future. I stopped being a victim and realized my control.

The ones who get this play longer. When the game is over they move into something else: coaching, business, life. People still listen.

Cultivating Patience

Too Ready, Too Soon

Illinois had our number in the early 90s. That 1990 game was no different, tension was high all week. Their defense didn't just tackle you, they punished you. Every carry came with two or three helmets trying to knock the ball loose, and your head off your body at the same time.

Juice had a rough start. A couple of missed reads. Runs that usually popped weren't hitting. Coach T grabbed me between drives and said it flat:

"We're leaning on you now."

This was it, the moment I'd replayed in my mind a thousand times.

I ran through Illinois like I had something personal to prove. Lowered the boom. Bounced off linebackers. Ripped off chunk plays. We didn't win, but I walked off the field with my first 100-yard game and zero doubt that I was ready. Certified. The moment came, and I answered.

In my mind, that was the turning point.

Next week: Indiana.

Not only did I not start... I got fewer carries than I'd had in the five games before it.

I was sick.

Not angry in a loud way, just sick. Quietly stunned at how fast they dimmed the light again.

Then came the talk, coaches, media, teammates:

"You're doing great for a freshman." "Your time's coming." "Be happy you're contributing."

Nah. I wasn't here to contribute. I was here to take over.

They wanted me to smile and sit back like it wasn't my time yet, even after I showed them it was. Like I should be grateful just to be in the huddle, even though I'd just carried the team.

The kind of patience that wears you down and dares you to call it growth. It felt like punishment. Pretending you're okay being overlooked. Pretending you're not already ready.

That week tested me in a different way. I had to hold the line. Stay focused. Not lash out or spiral. I had to play the long game with short-game frustration bubbling under the surface.

Because sometimes, you're already ready. They have to be ready to see you.

Stop Following Someone Else's Map

Carlos Snow was the measuring stick.

At that point, he was the most talented running back I'd ever seen up close. Breakaway speed. Low center of gravity. He could take contact without losing balance. I remember reading a Sports Illustrated piece on him and Emmitt Smith, two freshmen being called the best backs in the country. Carlos had broken the national high school record with over 100 touchdowns. His talent was undeniable.

He was that guy, even in a locker room full of D1 athletes.

Every chance I got, I studied him. At 5'7" he had this compact violence to his style. He didn't shake you. He just ran through you. A fast bowling ball with a nasty burst and enough top-end speed to leave DBs behind. I wanted that. I wanted to move like him, finish like him, make the same plays he did.

And for a while, I tried.

I tried to match his path. Tried to match his game. I wanted my rise to mirror his. Not just because I respected him, but because success looked like that to me.

It took me longer than I'd like to admit to realize I wasn't him. I wasn't built like him. And trying to run his race was slowing down my own.

That realization stung at first. You admire someone that much, and you want to believe if you just put in that work, you'll get the same result. But your game is your game. I had to stop chasing his blueprint and start trusting mine.

Carlos showed me what greatness looked like. But chasing his rise almost made me miss my own.

That realization hit me hard. I'd blown valuable time chasing their timeline when I should've been building mine.

You don't find your way by copying someone else's route. You find it by walking yours.

Overcoming Challenges to Patience

Same Depth Chart. Different Dude.

The scout team tests your patience like nothing else. You work harder than anyone, take more hits than the starters, and get none of the Saturday glory.

I walked back to my dorm with sore legs and a head full of questions. The building was quiet. The day was done. But something in me wasn't. I didn't know if the work was helping, but I wasn't ready to stop.

The doubt hit me deeper than just football. It made me question everything, my place at Ohio State, whether I really had what it took, if all this work would ever pay off. Walking back to my dorm with campus empty, nobody around to see me putting in the extra time, no validation coming my way, just me alone with my thoughts and choices.

I kept showing up each day, because it was the only thing I knew how to do. No lightning bolt moment. No big turning point. Just the daily grind of doing the work and coming back tomorrow. The habit of showing up kept me going. I needed to earn proof I could handle whatever came next. Nothing heroic about it, just stubbornness and knowing deep down this was my path, even when it felt like I was going nowhere.

To keep from going crazy, I started setting my own markers. How many days could I go full tilt in conditioning without letting up? Started with three. Got it up to two straight weeks. I'd study the Defense during scout team and test myself, could I read the front? Spot the stunt? I stopped going through the motions and started checking receipts. If I was getting better, I wanted proof.

I still remember a defensive coach losing it during practice. "You're getting your asses kicked by a scout team back, what the hell do you think Iowa's gonna do?" It was a backhanded compliment, but it landed. Nobody else might've cared, but I did. That was mine.

Those little wins were proof I was getting somewhere, I was still in the same spot on the depth chart, but I wasn't the same dude.

This was the rebirth of the Quiet Storm.

That Was Supposed to Be Me

The other running back in our '89 class was Dante Lee. Compact, maybe five-nine, 180 on a good day. They called him Quick and the name fit. Slick. Shifty. Hard to square up. I was built to run through people. He was built to make them miss.

Heading into camp I had the edge for the #3 spot behind Carlos and JB. I felt like I'd earned it. Then I turned my ankle and the door swung open. Dante ran right through it.

He played his ass off. Started a few big games, even got the nod in the Michigan matchup. By the end of the season he'd piled up over 500 yards and looked like the obvious starter for the next year. Meanwhile I was on the outside watching the thing I'd worked for slide into someone else's hands.

I didn't hate Quick. I liked the kid. But every time he ripped off a run or caught a compliment, something inside me tightened.

Not because he didn't deserve it. Because I thought it was supposed to be me.

That kind of jealousy is the worst. You can't point to logic. He wasn't showboating. He wasn't faking anything. He was just balling. And somewhere under everything, I started hoping he'd stumble. Not because I wanted him to fail, but because I needed proof that my shot still existed.

I kept telling myself the same lie: "Your time's coming." The more I said it, the less I believed it.

Coach Cooper had that stupid whistle-twirl and a song for Dante. He'd walk practice singing, "The greatest sight you'll ever see is giving the ball to Dante Lee." Guys laughed and half-sang along. I did too, on the outside. Inside it felt like salt in an open wound.

Then came the thing that cut the deepest.

One day, after a game, we were walking to the car. My Pops dropped it like a sucker punch. He said I was alright and then pointed at Dante. "He's my favorite. He's so quick and fun to watch. I love watching him." I don't have words for what that did to me. I'd been grinding my whole life for that one line, that small sound that meant I mattered to him. He gave it to my teammate.

He laughed like it was funny.

I said nothing. I nodded like it didn't sting. But the hurt sat in my ribs and stayed there every time I breathed. I'd waited my whole life to hear those words and he handed them to somebody else.

This was the quiet that changed the Storm.

Seen But Not Heard

One afternoon in my freshman year, I was in this small seminar class, mostly white students, a white professor. We were talking about politics and culture, and I said something, don't even remember exactly what, but it wasn't controversial. Just thoughtful. The kind of thing anyone might say in a class like that.

The professor stopped. Looked at me longer than necessary. And said, "Now, that's *actually* a really interesting point."

That *actually* caught me off balance.

I didn't say anything back. Just nodded like it didn't bother me. But inside, I felt it. The surprise in his voice. Like intelligence coming from me was unexpected. Like I jumped out of the script he'd already written for me.

And that wasn't a one-off.

Around campus, I was treated like a minor celebrity. People recognized me. Some wanted autographs. Some professors smiled more once they learned I played football. But in those same classrooms, I'd see the pause when I raised my hand. I'd feel the weight behind the stares. Like I was only supposed to be loud on Saturdays.

I found some peace in Black student groups. Those rooms were different. Nobody was shocked when I had something to say. I didn't have to prove I belonged, we just belonged.

The hardest part of being a Black athlete at a mostly white school was knowing how to switch gears without losing myself. I had to start learning patience with myself in a whole new way, that didn't come easy. Learning not to lose who I was on the field, in class, on High Street, in a study group, at a party. It was always a tightrope.

Patience was learning how to keep walking that line without growing bitter or losing my voice. I couldn't force people to see me clearly, but I could make damn sure I didn't disappear.

Success Story: Nelson Mandela

I'd been living inside my own waiting game, scout team and injuries eating at me, doubts creeping in daily. Then Mandela's story entered the picture and gave that waiting a new lens.

My Black Studies classes introduced me to Nelson Mandela during my early years at OSU, and his story flipped my understanding of patience.

Twenty-seven years. In prison. That's longer than most entire football careers. Hell, longer than most marriages. He gave up more than time. He missed birthdays. Funerals. The chance to hold his kids as they grew. Think about that. No career to fall back on. No guarantee of freedom. Just time, and the decision not to waste it.

They locked up the body, but they couldn't touch the mission. Quietly. Relentlessly. He studied the enemy.

Sharpened his mind. He built in silence, studying the same system that tried to break him. He learned Afrikaans, the language of the very people who put him there, because he knew freedom required readiness. He watched. He grew.

That part of his story really resonated. The world saw a prisoner. He was building a strategy behind those walls. Studying when nobody was watching. Preparing for a moment that might never come.

And when he got out? The leadership he showed after prison came directly from those invisible years. The foundation was built when nobody was watching. He was ready. Four years later, he became the first Black president of South Africa.

Mandela taught me patience means preparing while the world isn't watching. The outside world saw waiting. Inside, it was all work. He found purpose in the pause and came out with more power than he went in with.

Patience Conclusion: Built From the Wait

There's a version of patience that people love to talk about...This is not that version.

People love talking patience when it leads somewhere. This chapter wasn't that. This was getting stuck in your own head, watching your shot disappear. Telling yourself you're next while quietly wondering if that's even true.

Scout team tested me while nobody was looking. No cameras. No feedback. Just daily car crashes, and me limping back to the dorm wondering if any of it mattered. It didn't feel like growth. It felt like getting beat up and quickly forgotten.

Watching Juice take the carries I thought were mine forced me to sit with some feelings I wasn't ready for. He was balling. And I wanted to be happy for him, but it ate at me. Having my Pops say my teammate was his favorite? That truly hurt my heart.

These moments stung, but I stayed anyway.

I kept going. I kept grinding. Somewhere in that stretch, I started to change. I just stayed in it long enough for something solid to take shape.

It wasn't what I pictured, and it damn sure wasn't clean. But it was the realest moment I ever had.

Nobody tells you that patience might feel like failure while it's working. That you might not even notice it's working. You're just stuck in it, trying not to let go.

Those quiet stretches, the ones that felt like nothing was happening, ended up building the strongest parts of me. No celebration. No breakthrough. You don't get the Storm overnight. You build it in the quiet.

EMPowered to Act: Your Patience Playbook

Find Your People: Scout team was hard, but the guys I trusted kept me from slipping. Your turn: who's walking a similar path? Don't wait for motivation. Build accountability. Pick two or three people you can check in with, keep it real, and hold each other up when the frustration hits.

Keep Your Own Score: Nobody was clapping for me in those early days, so I kept my own stats, calling out blitzes, finishing runs. You? Track something that shows you're growing, even if nobody else sees it yet. The progress is real even when the praise doesn't follow.

Use the Competition: The "stable" could've crushed my confidence. Instead, I studied the others. What's one person who seems ahead of you right now? Learn from them. Borrow what works, leave what doesn't. Their success doesn't block yours. It can sharpen it.

The only permission you need is your own. Never forget: Patience is 100% in your control.

CHAPTER 3

COMMITMENT: THE LINE BETWEEN INTEREST AND INVESTMENT

COMMITMENT is the third cornerstone of our **MINDSET** controls. It's where the real ones separate from the pretenders. Where you find out who's showing up when the lights are off and nobody's watching.

"You're not committed. You're just interested."

Coach Kennedy's words hit like a gut punch. I sat there stunned while he slid the attendance sheet across the desk, absences highlighted in "Gotcha Yellow."

The fluorescent lights buzzed overhead, making the silence between us even heavier. I could feel it, the intensity coming off him. He leaned in, eyes locked on mine, daring me to look away.

I'd walked in ready to explain why I was transferring. Why I deserved better. Why the new offensive coordinator didn't understand my game. Why I was too good to be blocking for somebody else.

Coach K didn't give a damn about any of that.

He just held up a mirror.

"Listen to yourself," he said. "Interested people do what's convenient. They show up when it's easy. Quit when it's not. Committed people? They find a way. They get it done, no matter how they feel."

Then he stood up, maybe 5'7" on paper, but towering like a giant in the moment.

"I watch you every day. You're just a guy. You're average. Good luck at your next school."

And he walked out.

Left me sitting there. Alone with the truth I didn't want to hear.

After a season full of headlines, 100-yard games, touchdowns, my name buzzing everywhere, I thought I had arrived.

Then the new offense hit. New position. Running back to fullback. Star to grunt. Glory to ghost.

Instead of handling it like a G, I whined and complained like a big ass baby. Rolled my eyes in meetings. Dogged it in blocking drills. Told myself I was still "committed to the game," just not to this role they were forcing on me.

That season broke me because I wasn't committed enough to handle it mentally.

I went through the motions. Gave half effort.

In football, partial effort gets you hurt.

In life, it leaves you stuck wondering why the doors you knock on don't open.

I thought I was a beast.

I was really just another bullshit guy.

That twelve-minute conversation exposed me and ultimately saved me. I sat in that office long after he left, hoping nobody else would walk in.

I felt raw and exposed. He never raised his voice. The truth wasn't loud. It just sat there quiet, steady and undeniable.

I tried to shake it off and comfort my ego by calling it politics. I really wanted to be mad and blame him for being another coach that didn't get me.

But those absences were real. That attitude in meetings? That was real too. The effort I thought I gave, I knew it wasn't full.

After sitting with it, football wasn't the real issue. It forced me to confront the gap between who I said I was and how I actually showed up. It's like a funhouse mirror, it doesn't show your reflection, it exposes your patterns.

We all carry a version of ourselves we like to believe in. We say we're committed. We say we're built different. But when it's uncomfortable, when it's inconvenient, our actions tell the real story.

Coach Kennedy held that mirror up for me. But we all get those moments. A teammate calling out your effort. A partner who's tired of the excuses. Or that quiet feeling when you're alone and can't lie to yourself anymore.

Grown-man commitment starts when the performance ends. When you stop defending what you meant to do and start owning what you actually did.

That day dared me to become somebody else. Somebody who didn't need the spotlight and could carry anything.

No one was coming to explain it. I had to figure out what commitment looked like when there was nothing left to prove, just something to live.

If you're not ready to pay in full, you'll stay average, even when you're talented.

Understanding Commitment

That second year tested me. The numbers were solid. I was contributing. But none of it felt stable. And when the new coordinator came in and moved me to fullback, that confirmed it.

I didn't want to block. Didn't sign up to be a role player. But I told myself I was still committed, just not to that.

Over time, I saw three levels of it, on the field, off it, everywhere. And most people never get past the first.

Surface Commitment: Conditional Loyalty

I used to think commitment meant staying late and playing hard. But I was still only 'in' while I was 'gettin' mine.' Because I showed up early and did the drills when the cameras were off.

But looking back, that wasn't commitment. That was conditional loyalty.

As long as the role made me feel important, I was in. As long as I was producing, I gave full energy. But the second my spot got questioned or the offense didn't feature me the way I thought it should, I withdrew. Quietly at first, less eye contact in meetings, lighter finishes in drills, but it was there.

It's pride that says, 'I'll give my best, if I still feel like the man.' It's when you confuse talent for buy-in, and attention for value. You're still doing the work, but only as long as it fits your picture of how things should go.

I was dependable...until it got uncomfortable.

Strategic Commitment: Quiet Room. Loud Work.

After that sit-down with Coach Kennedy, the mirror cracked. I'd been pouting like a grown man hiding in a boy's mindset. Telling myself I was "handling business," when in reality, I was shrinking.

Right there, I flipped.

Not emotional. Straight tactical.

I decided to treat commitment like a job, concentrating on execution. I felt discouraged at times, but I kept showing up. I started training harder. Blocking without eye rolls. Taking pride in technique. Running those extra gassers even when I hated the damn reason I was running them.

It still stung to be in the background, but I learned to keep going, even when it felt like nobody gave a damn.

You're doing the unglamorous work alone, and still bitter over the role you didn't want. It's the decision to stay steady when everything inside you wants to buckle. To build something even when folks are only looking at the finished product.

I didn't love the role. But I started to love what it was building in me.

Transformative Commitment: Identity Over Ego

Eventually, it stopped feeling like sacrifice. No need to act. No need to prove. I just was.

At this point the internal scoreboard turned off. No more obsessing over the praise or carries. I quit tracking who stood ahead of me on the depth chart. The work became the reward. I showed up to everything, weight room, film study, all of it, with a completely different mindset. Carrying the weight of a choice I didn't need to explain.

You know commitment has transformed you when the outcomes stop driving the effort, and you keep showing up anyway.

You still want more, but you stop needing someone else's permission to give your all.

By the time spring ball came around, I was back at running back. But something had transformed. I brought something different to the position, everything I earned in the storm that nobody else saw.

Importance of Commitment

Commitment isn't a declaration.

It's what holds when life moves faster than your plan. Because in football, and life, your circumstances will change. Your role will shift. Your body will break. The system won't wait.

You will get tested. The question is: what's going to stay true when everything else doesn't?

Physical Challenges: Proof in the Sweat

You can't hide in this sport. I grew up on Walter Payton and Earl Campbell, I modeled my game after them. No juking. Just damage.

Some guys talked. The real ones were already sweating. Morning workouts before classes. Extra reps beyond what my card said to do. Studying playbooks during downtime. Getting treatment before anyone else showed up. The stuff nobody saw made the stuff everybody talked about.

Once I saw what I was doing, I couldn't keep lying to myself. I stayed after and caught passes to improve my hands. Made it a point to run routes, so the QBs would trust me as a legit option. I even grabbed some of the younger LB's to make the routes more realistic.

The result? I transformed my role and went from the #3 FB to the #1 RB in one offseason. That shit never happens. Nothing changed in my body. Everything changed in my mind and that changed my future.

Interest costs...investment pays.

Mental Challenges: Too Many Rooms

The mental battle was worse than the physical. During my redshirt year, I crushed school because football demands were light. But once I started playing, class stopped feeling as important. I wanted to be great at both. But my head couldn't stay in the room. In class? I was running option routes in my head. At practice? My mind was on what I had to deal with at home.

My high school girlfriend was pregnant. She and my daughter moved to Columbus. We were living together. I wasn't just a student-athlete anymore, I was a father. Trying to do three full-time jobs at once. And I didn't know what the hell I was doing at any of them.

Coaches talked academics like they mattered. But you knew what they really cared for. Professors didn't care when you had a game. Didn't matter how full your plate was, just make sure it's empty before tomorrow.

I kept showing up, but I was never fully there. Not in the classroom. Not on the field. Not at home.

Commitment really means being fully present wherever you are. Not going through the motions and hoping it works out. Because when your mind's all over the place, your game will be too.

Relationship Challenges: No Love When It's Ugly

Rebuilding trust is harder when you're the one who dropped the ball. I had to learn that the long way.

Teams aren't families. They're collections of guys trying to survive. Cliques form fast, by position, by class, by where you're from. Stars get treated one way. Walk-ons another. Coaches swear they're fair, but everybody knows that ain't true.

Some teammates doubted my renewed commitment after the awakening. Some were skeptical of the sudden change. And a few? They flat-out enjoyed watching me struggle.

I don't blame them. I hadn't exactly earned the benefit of the doubt. I was loud when things were good and quiet when they weren't. I had to own that before anybody could trust me again.

Meanwhile, I had to maintain other critical relationships outside football. Professors who determined whether I passed classes. Athletic Trainers who influenced my playing status. Each relationship demanded authentic commitment rather than superficial interaction.

Anyone can show love when it's easy. The real ones show up when disappointment and ego get in the way.

Career Challenges: System Don't Wait

Football squeezes a lifetime's worth of pressure into four years. No rewrites. No mulligans. Every practice, every game, someone's coming for your spot. And your future? It's sitting in the hands of coaches with agendas you'll never fully see.

One day, I'm learning a new position. Next day, some five-star recruit's standing in the room. Then the coordinator gets swapped out, and the whole playbook flips. Everything you thought made you valuable gets questioned.

They say they believe in development. But trust me, they're always hunting for your replacement. Every year. Every recruiting cycle. They're looking for a younger version of you with less attitude and more upside.

You feel it, this low-key pressure to prove you still matter. And sometimes it ain't even low-key.

The easy move? Transfer. Blame the system.

The harder move? Redefine your value. Find ways to matter again.

I had to stop waiting for the system to validate me and start finding ways to force their hand.

Talent might catch attention. But if you don't back it up with commitment, that attention fades fast.

Cultivating Commitment

From Wake-Up to Buy-In

The wake-up call stripped away my excuses. I'd been blaming coaches and schemes for my move to fullback, but I was finally forced to see it for what it really was: half-assed effort. I wasn't committed to excellence. I was just interested in success.

Interest asks, "What can I get?" Commitment asks, "What can I build?"

That flipped how I saw hard. Before, tough moments felt like a reason to pull back. After? They became chances to separate.

The drills I used to survive? I started attacking them. I stayed after to run routes and catch passes. I also learned that better questions got better answers. My present was investing in my future.

During practice one day, something unlocked inside me. I started seeing opportunities and angles I'd completely missed before. Foot placement. Timing. When to press the hole and when to bounce it. The reads I used to force started feeling smoother and more natural.

What clicked was this, growth stacks in layers, not leaps. Clean up the details first, then watch the game slow down around you. Your vision transforms with experience. No shortcuts, just unglamorous work that pays off when it matters most.

I stopped obsessing over where I stood and started tracking how I moved.

I didn't chase the scoreboard. I built the thing the scoreboard couldn't see.

I Saw It. I Didn't Claim It.

I watched "The Game" of '89 from the sidelines. Scottie Graham's performance was the most complete display I'd ever seen from a running back. Stakes were high. Carlos was out with an injury. And Scottie didn't flinch. He ran dives, counters, sweeps, screens...from fullback and tailback. Same motion. Different job. Play after play. He ran through the Wolverines like they weren't the best defense in the Big Ten. A grown man on every snap.

The whole stadium felt it. His game went beyond yards or toughness. He dominated with control and versatility. He became whatever the team needed, exactly when we needed it. And the offense rode his back the whole way.

I was in awe.

And here's the wild part: I was so locked in on being a tailback, I never saw myself in that role.

I had the size. The strength. The vision. But I couldn't see it yet. That moment should've shown me I could've been that hybrid. That "Ultra Back" I later became in the league? Scottie was already doing it. The blueprint was sitting right in front of me.

But back then? I just couldn't see it.

I'm still stunned when I think back on that day. Not just the game he played, but how long it took me to realize I was capable of the same thing. And more.

Sometimes the hardest part isn't becoming it, it's seeing it. Recognizing what's already in you before someone hands you permission. I didn't. I was still holding on to what I used to be, so I couldn't see what I was ready to become.

It didn't click until years later. But when it did? That change reshaped my whole career.

Overcoming Challenges to Commitment

Success Made Me Soft

Success will mess with your head faster than failure ever could. After my breakout season, the

"Quiet Storm" was making noise. I wasn't the man yet. But I felt like I was HIM. That feeling? Setup

I didn't slack off, not outright. But something in me got comfortable. I'd proven myself. Coaches knew what I could do. I wasn't grinding with the same desperation. I still worked, but I wasn't as hungry.

It happens quietly, the student who coasts after one good semester. The business that gets hot and stops pushing. The couple that gets comfortable and lets the fire fade. Success tricks you into thinking you've arrived, when really, all it's done is raise the standard for what's next.

Coach K saw it, and then he helped me see it. I wasn't competing against my teammates. Or the coaches. Or the system.

I was competing against myself.

And I was losing.

The ones who dominate after that first taste of success never settle for just protecting what they built. They keep expanding territory while others get comfortable. Every day they walk in like they still have everything to prove, even with trophies already on the shelf.

You can admire the mountain you climbed, or you can keep climbing. But you can't do both.

Old Eyes, New You

If my style made you uncomfortable, that's on you. I brought a whole different presence to campus. Militant. People called it that. African beads. X-Clan in my Walkman. I didn't eat pork.

Boycotted Nikes. Wore red, black, and green like it was armor. I walked around carrying something way heavier than books and my playbook.

I wasn't the most approachable. I wasn't a warm guy. And I didn't care.

Back then, I wasn't always sure if I was standing for something...or just pushing people away. I judged everything. My circle was tight, and I made quick calls on who was down and who wasn't. It's hard to be a good teammate when you're trying to be a part-time revolutionary. I wasn't a problem, but I wasn't easy either.

Fast forward. Something had to give.

When I started changing my choices, doing extra work, leading in drills, conditioning, watching film on purpose, speaking up in meetings, embracing critiques, rooting on my guys, asking for help, showing love...

I knew I was growing. But I didn't expect what came with it.

We were in the middle of winter workouts, bear crawls across the WHAC field. The turf smelled like rubber and sweat. Everybody was forked. I tried to hype up one of the younger guys to push through.

"Oh, now you're a leader?"

Said it low. But it landed.

I chuckled, because it was fair. He was being honest. He was right. I hadn't earned his trust yet. Not from him. Not from most of them.

It's easier to train your body than it is to rebuild how people see you.

Just because you believe in the new you doesn't mean they do. That part takes time. And receipts. That's a whole different kind of test.

Can you keep showing up as the new you, even when they're still seeing the old one?

Not for approval. Not to win them over.

Just because this is who you are now...regardless of who they still see.

This Ain't What I Signed Up For

That sophomore year I had to weather a different storm. Nobody questioned my spot in the offense anymore. Coaches called my number when the game was on the line. Media waited for sound bites after games. My name meant something when I walked through campus.

Then I got hurt.

And just like that, I went from a focal point to a footnote. Depth chart? Bottom. Reporters? Gone. Even getting on the field felt like a long shot.

My response? Blame everybody but myself, the one thing I couldn't control. Trainers rushed me back too soon. Coaches weren't calling the right plays. I sat in meetings making slick comments under my breath, acting like I saw the game clearer than the guys coaching it.

I didn't realize it at the time, but I was fighting for the identity I thought I'd earned.

The mirror showed up during film study. There I was, half-stepping through "inside" drills, going full speed only when the lights were on, then wondering why I wasn't getting reps.

That old saying was still true: "The tape don't lie."

I could finally see it, how I was sabotaging myself while blaming everybody else.

Sometimes leadership shows up as a hug. Sometimes it shows up as a moment of clarity.

One of our senior leaders pulled me aside after practice.

"You're better than this shit you're putting out," he said.

"I don't care if you're hurt. I don't care if you're pissed. But I do care that you're wasting what you got. Either be here, or don't. This halfway shit? Not good enough."

That line stuck in my head the rest of the season. On a daily basis, I'd have to ask myself: "Are you here or not?" Some days the answer was stronger than others. But asking the question forced me to name my commitment, no more sleepwalking through the frustration.

I'd dug the hole so deep I didn't know how to climb out. I did what a lot of people do when they're drowning in their own choices: I didn't try to fix it. I just looked for an escape.

I decided to transfer. The easy exit looked better than the hard work. Running seemed simpler than rebuilding.

If Coach K hadn't called me out, I might've spent my whole career running from one team to the next, one situation to another, never realizing that I was actually... running from myself.

This Game Was Rigged

College football came with terms nobody could ever explain. Transfer rules punished the players, but not the coaches. Academic demands clashed with practice. Millions flowed through the program, but we saw none of it. Then we got a new running backs coach who had never played or coached the position.

I remember sitting in meetings wondering how this dude was going to make me better. He barely spoke our language. But I kept my face straight and nodded along like it made sense.

I saw how other guys handled it. Some coasted through. Others were always angry. Then there were the ones who broke the rules on purpose, just to feel like they still had a little control.

If I'm being honest, I tried all of it. One week I'd be sulking through drills, giving off just enough energy to not get singled out. The next, I'd be skipping study tables or walk-throughs like it was some act of protest. Telling myself it was all bullshit. That I was better than this.

But deep down, I was fooling myself while hiding inside the system. I didn't want to grind through something I didn't believe in. I didn't want to commit if I wasn't sure I'd get rewarded. I thought the whole thing was rigged, and maybe it was, but that didn't make how I handled it any less weak.

"Eventually I realized the setup wasn't going to change. Staying mad wouldn't fix it. Coasting wasn't helping. I had to find a way to show up anyway. Commitment started meaning something else, when showing up got harder. Nothing changed in the system. But commitment stopped depending on fairness. It turned into a line I wasn't willing to cross anymore.

When Coach asked who wanted extra film study, I started being the first hand up, not because the system deserved it, but because I did."

I started getting to film early. Stayed late breaking down opponents. My notes got sharper. I started asking better questions. Nobody was watching that part. But it started changing me, long before it changed my spot.

Success Story: Muhammad Ali

If you want to see commitment in its rawest form, look at Muhammad Ali when the world stripped him of everything he had worked for.

Ali was on top, undefeated, heavyweight champion, a global icon. Then came the Vietnam draft. He refused, standing on his faith: "I ain't got no quarrel with them Vietcong."

The system tried to break him. Took his title. Snatched his license. Cut him off from the one thing that made him who he was. At twenty-five years old, right in his prime, he was locked out of the ring, stripped of everything he'd fought for.

Most athletes would've folded and put their career over conviction. Ali didn't flinch. "I'd rather be in jail for standing up for what I believe than be free knowing I didn't stand for something."

For three and a half years, he couldn't throw a punch. But he didn't stay quiet. He traveled to colleges, spoke his truth, even when the rooms didn't want to hear it. He sharpened his voice. He built something bigger than belts and trophies. He stopped being just a fighter and became a force.

By 1970, he was reinstated, but the game had changed. New champions. New styles. His first fight back? A loss to Joe Frazier. Ali was slower and lost key development years.

That prime window? Gone. But he didn't waste time sitting in regret. He rebuilt his whole game to fit who he was now and made that version just as dangerous.

Ali reinvented himself. He couldn't float like before, so he found new ways to win, mastering mind games, developing strategies like "rope-a-dope." In 1974, against all odds, he took back the heavyweight title, beating George Foreman in the legendary "Rumble in the Jungle."

Ali's story cuts deep for me. Different stage, same truth underneath.

I wasn't fighting for history like Ali was. I wasn't risking my freedom. But in my small world at Ohio State, it felt like everything I worked for was on the line. And in my little corner of the storm, I learned what standing tall in hard moments really looked like.

I faced a position change that stripped away how I saw myself. He faced exile from the very sport that made him who he was.

I had to find new ways to stay alive as a fullback. He had to rebuild everything, his body, his style, his whole approach, just to keep fighting.

Commitment is when the old plan gets ripped up and you don't fold. You find a way forward without losing yourself.

Ali rebuilt his legacy in real time. And that's why he didn't just remain a champion. He became immortal.

Commitment Conclusion: Commitment Ain't Clean

Before, hard moments felt like reasons to pull back. After that turn, they became opportunities to push deeper. The conditioning drills I used to coast through became battles I needed to win, because every one of them helped rebuild who I was. I wasn't just getting through it anymore. I was taking something back.

Commitment shows up when quitting makes sense, and nobody would blame you for doing it. When the excuses sound good. When nobody would blame you for walking away. The real truth shows up when the plan's blown up and you have to decide if you're still in.

That meeting in Coach K's office made it plain. Exposed the gap between who I thought I was and how I'd actually been showing up. Same thing with Ali when they tried to strip everything from him. Commitment shows in what you do when the fight gets ugly, and staying in it starts to cost you.

The core of this chapter? It's what you hold onto when everything's gone sideways.

Begin your commitment assessment today: Where are you interested, and where are you truly committed? What are you controlling, and what's controlling you?

EMPowered to Act: Your Commitment Playbook

Hold Yourself to a Standard - Every morning after Coach K lit me up, I asked myself one thing: "Are you here or not?" Your move: Find your version of that question. One that rattles your core every day, not pats you on the back. It should make you answer, not hide. No halfway showing up. No disappearing when it counts.

Build the Walls Around It - Motivation fades. To survive, I built walls around my time and focus, made sure slipping wasn't even an option. Your move: Pick one place where you keep slipping. Set the time. Set the standard. No decisions left to make when the moment hits. It's already done.

Outgrow the Old Version - After my mindset changed, not everybody bought in. Some teammates still saw the guy who used to coast or complain. And I couldn't blame them. Your move: Just keep showing up. Keep doing the work until the new version becomes undeniable. You rebuild trust without asking for it. Quiet receipts. Day after day.

Flip the Threat - When they moved me to fullback, I saw it as a demotion. I made it a weapon. Your move: What's testing you right now? Ask yourself: How does this make me harder to break? Turn the hit into fuel. The only way to stay in it when life changes the script is to rewrite your role.

So many fold when commitment gets expensive.

The ones who change the game? They lean in harder when the road gets ugly.

Circumstances don't choose that. You do.

Never forget: Commitment is 100% in your control.

CHAPTER 4

POSITIVITY: HARD-EARNED

POSITIVITY is the fourth cornerstone of our **MINDSET** controls. It's what you reach for when the weight hits, and nobody's handing you an easy way out.

Three weeks before the start of the season. One wrong cut. One loud pop.

Flat on my back, body stuck in shock. I couldn't hear a thing. The whole season I'd built in my head ended right there. I was just another guy stuck in the training room while the team moved on.

It wasn't the physical rehab that gutted me. Rehab was basic: ice, stretch, lift, repeat. That part didn't bother me. What messed with me was how fast I started disappearing. Coaches stopped checking in. Teammates kept it moving. I'd hear them laughing across the locker room, and I wasn't even part of the convo anymore. It felt like being erased.

Positivity at that point had nothing to do with smiling or pretending I was good. It damn sure wasn't about hype.

Positivity meant staying in it. Showing up even though I didn't trust my leg and every step was a sharp reminder that I wasn't right.

Staying connected when it was easier to fade out entirely. Finding new ways to be valuable, even when everything I imagined for myself was now out of reach. Finding some way, any way, to still matter, even when everything I pictured for myself was slipping away.

Fast forward to the Illinois game.

Crowd still buzzing from the final whistle. Boos coming down heavy as we walked toward the tunnel, arm around Eddie's shoulders. I felt him sinking under the weight: two costly fumbles that lost the game and painted him as the goat. And I'm not talking about the 'Greatest Of All Time.'

One fan leaned over the railing, face twisted with rage, spit flying, breath soaked in beer, screaming, "You suck Eddie!"

I felt my own fists tighten but held back. Eddie just kept walking: eyes down, shoulders slumped, that 6'3" frame shrinking like he was trying to disappear. Same fans who were chanting "Ed-die! Ed-die!" a week ago were now spitting venom in his direction like he never mattered. He didn't say a word. Didn't need to. He knew exactly what was waiting.

I pulled him closer. "They're gonna blame this L on you."

He didn't answer, didn't look up. Didn't need to.

"But that shit doesn't define you," I said. "It's what you do next. You've got two options. Let this break you, or make it your fuel. It's up to you man."

It was the same survival guide I'd just written for myself the hard way. Now I was handing it to my brother who needed it.

Most folks get positivity all twisted. They think it's just smiling and pretending nothing's wrong. Calling it positivity doesn't make it real. It's just denial dressed up to look strong.

Grounded positivity shows up when everything around you is trying to shut you down. It doesn't pretend the weight ain't there. It just carries it a different way.

There was nothing fake about walking through that tunnel with Eddie. We felt the loss. We heard the boos. But we weren't letting that moment write the next chapter.

So many get stuck there: They mistake facing pain for giving in to it. Like if you admit it hurts, it's over. They dress it up with a fake smile and call it strength.

But that kind of surface positivity always breaks. One hit and it crumbles.

The real kind? The kind that lasts? It doesn't dodge reality. It changes your posture inside it. It says, "Yeah, this happened. Now what am I gonna do with it?

Strength lives there. The hard work nobody sees but you. The kind that gets done whether anyone notices or not.

The kind that walks through a storm so public and brutal it would break most people, yet never folds.

Eddie didn't hide. He lifted his head and didn't make excuses. He faced it head on.

And I realized: this ain't weakness. This is power most people will never understand.

Because sometimes, you're the one learning it from the sideline. Sometimes, you're the one teaching it, telling a brother to walk tall when the world wants him to crawl.

Understanding Positivity

People stop trusting positivity because they've only seen the fake kind. The kind that melts the second life pushes back. But positivity has levels. You earn it by surviving what breaks others. You build it to stay upright when everything else falls out.

Surface Positivity: Good on Paper

This is the positivity that only works when things are going your way.

At Ohio State, I saw teammates with slogans taped to their lockers and T-shirts that say Big TEAM little me. They'd shut down anyone voicing concerns in team meetings, calling it "negative energy." Their confidence seemed unshakable.

Then reality would hit. A demotion on the depth chart. An injury. A tough loss. Whatever it was, when real weight landed, that surface positivity vanished.

Guys would tear ligaments and immediately start with "God's plan" and "everything happens for a reason." Plenty of comeback talk in the locker room. But in the training facility? Missing rehab sessions. Rushing protocols. Dodging hard conversations with trainers. Their "positivity" became a shield that prevented them from doing the real work: facing the injury honestly and rebuilding methodically.

Other teammates took a different approach. No slogans. No performance. Just acknowledgment of where things stood. "This is where I am today." Showing up consistently. Asking uncomfortable questions. Facing every measurement. Not pretending it didn't hurt, but moving forward through it.

One approach sounded better. The other actually built something.

Surface positivity works until it doesn't. It's cheap paint over weak materials. It looks fine until pressure hits, then cracks everywhere.

The guys who succeeded weren't always the most talented. They were the ones who could face reality without flinching, then keep building anyway. Genuine positivity is choosing to move forward when nothing feels positive.

Strategic Positivity: Beyond Just Coachable

I'd just put up another big game and still felt like a failure.

Coach T didn't let anything slide. If my angle was off or my footwork got lazy, he lit me up. Didn't matter how many points I scored, he stayed on me like I'd fumbled ten times.

That day, I stayed behind. A little irritated, but more confused.

"I thought I played well," I said. "You did," he said. "Which is exactly why I'm so hard on you."

At first, I couldn't hear it. Still felt like criticism. Still had that urge to explain myself. I grew up around yelling. Around power trips dressed up as coaching. I thought this was just more of that.

It took a while, but I started to see it: he expected more. What felt like tearing me down was really just investment.

That changed everything.

I stopped running from feedback. Started looking for the coaches who shot me straight, because I realized the criticism was constructive and they were betting on me.

It still stung. But that sting meant I mattered. That somebody still gave a damn whether I got better or not.

No more just keeping a good attitude. I was learning how to lead. Hungrier. More open. And coaches don't miss that. When a coach starts rooting for you, not just coaching you, that becomes the turning point. It's the move from getting coached... to being believed in.

Transformative Positivity: Legacy Over Stats

The highest level of positivity builds something strong enough to lift everybody around you.

At Ohio State, our running back room was stacked: By'not'e, Juice, Eddie, Jeff Cothran, me. All killers. The competition was real. Everybody wanted touches. Everybody wanted to shine.

But that room? It was still The Brotherhood.

This wasn't pretend, we actually had each other's backs. We pushed each other because we knew the value of competition, and we were actually rooting for each other.

Before heading to the league, Scottie Graham dropped a line that stuck with me:

"If you help everyone in this room get better, the coaches will have no choice but to find ways to get us all on the field."

That line reset everything.

There were moments I wanted more. When someone else broke a big run through a huge hole, I felt that twinge. I was happy for them, but I wanted mine too. That feeling could've pulled me off track if I let it.

But I didn't. I'd dap them up. I'd break down what I saw, even if it meant they got the spotlight before I did.

And secretly? I was growing too.

That mindset made us sharper, and tighter. We were building trust. And that trust made us dangerous. The coaches saw it. We all got chances. And we became one of the best backfields in the country. We always had the talent, but now the egos didn't kill our chemistry.

I kept giving what I knew away, because the standard mattered more than the spotlight. Because when you make the whole room better, they find ways to keep you in the mix.

The energy you bring shapes the environment. And when the team gets better, you get better.

Simple as that.

Importance of Positivity

Positivity requires seeing reality clearly while finding strength to keep moving forward. It's how you move through pain without letting it define you. It's the muscle that lets you stay open, when everything in you wants to shut down.

The strongest people I knew weren't the loudest. They were the ones who didn't get stuck. They kept moving forward, trusting anyway.

When the Body Fights Itself

A sports psychologist once told me: "Your brain doesn't know the difference between a real threat and one you made up." I didn't want to believe it. But my body did.

Every step in rehab felt like a fight with something invisible. Even when the pain was gone, my body flinched like it was still coming. Trainers said "Relax." But my nervous system said, "Protect."

I had to do everything slow: basic movements. Heel slides. Glute bridges. Wall sits. Things I could've done in my sleep before. I had to stay loose when every instinct screamed at me to grip harder.

You could see the difference: The ones who stayed positive stayed present. They kept playing. Kept learning. The others? Stuck in their own bodies. Stayed stuck in fear.

One day, our head trainer grabbed my shoulders, looked me dead in the eyes, and said: "You're not fighting the injury anymore. You're fighting yourself."

That line stayed with me.

Real positivity builds quietly through daily battles inside your own head. No fanfare. Just breathing through the tightness. Just showing up. Trusting that you're still built for it, even when your body isn't so sure.

When the Praise Gets Loud

When you're losing, people expect you to stay positive. When you're winning? They don't warn you how dangerous that can be.

At Ohio State, when things started clicking, everything changed. Folks who barely noticed me before suddenly had endless smiles and handshakes. Classmates. Reporters. Even a few in my circle started treating me different.

It felt good, at first.

Then I noticed how fast it flipped. One bad game and the chatter changed. Same people. Different tune.

I remember walking into a film session after a loss. Nobody said a word. Same coaches who'd been praising me two weeks earlier didn't even look up. That silence said more than any breakdown could.

The moment I realized: If I let the crowd decide my value, I'd lose myself trying to earn something I never controlled.

That question became my anchor, every week, win or lose: Did you stand on what you said today?

Some days the answer was yes. Some days, no. But it kept me honest. Anchored.

I focused on my own standard instead of chasing praise or running from criticism.

The real positivity builds when you choose your identity over whatever image others try to create for you.

When the People You Love Don't See You

Nobody tells you how lonely it gets, even when you're surrounded.

In those days, we didn't have cell phones. No social media or FaceTime. Long-distance calls cost money I didn't have. You got ten minutes on Sundays if your phone card balance was right.

When pressure built up, I sat with it, alone.

But even if I could've reached out, who would've understood?

Nobody in my family had been here before. Not in D1 football. Not on a campus this big. Not in this world.

My dad was tough to talk to even when things were calm. My brother was gone. My sister was treading water in her own life. And the youngest one? Still a baby.

I wasn't angry. I felt something colder: distance. I had family members who sat in the stands on my tickets, then left without finding me after the game. How do you take a free seat and not stay for the person you came to see? Fam's tricky like that. They can love you deep and still miss who you are.

I didn't have the words. How do you explain carrying expectations nobody ever showed you?

In the end, I carried it myself.

It's quiet work. You do it alone. One day you look up and realize you needed it more than you knew.

Cultivating Positivity

Seen but Not Understood

I wasn't the only one learning how to hold steady through setbacks. I watched someone close live it in real time, and it stuck with me.

Not everybody who gets written off is built to rewrite the story. Eddie George was.

When he first got to Ohio State, he didn't carry himself like some big-time recruit. He just showed up and kept working. Biggest back I've ever seen, no doubt. 6'3", 225, but quiet. Almost too quiet. That FUMA military background gave him discipline most freshmen didn't have. He was respectful and soaked up everything around him. But because he wasn't flashy or chasing attention, some of the guys assumed he didn't have it.

Then came his breakout. That crazy three-TD game against Syracuse. Suddenly, everybody was talking like he was next up.

And just as fast? It turned.

A few costly fumbles that cost us the Illinois game. The trust from coaches dipped. The whispers started. And almost overnight, the same teammates who used to hype him up started saying things like, "He's too stiff" and "He runs too high." The hate and judgment were all in whispers. Like Eddie couldn't hear it. But he did. We all did.

He spent the rest of the year buried on the depth chart as an afterthought.

That would've crushed a lot of players. Especially someone young. You start questioning yourself. Start playing scared and shrinking to fit the version people expect.

But Eddie didn't shrink. He went internal and kept working. Never blamed the O-Line. Never lashed out. He chose positivity. Day after day, rep after rep, without promises of the future.

By the next season, he was third string and special teams. Still quiet. Still catching stray comments from guys saying the new 5-star RB or the fast guy out of FL was better. But underneath? That quiet kid was loading up.

He worked his way back. No pouting. No switch up. He just stayed centered and consistent.

When Eddie's shot came, he answered it. Against the same Illinois team that had broken us his freshman year, he went for over 300 yards. That game sealed his legacy and carried him to the Heisman Trophy.

Eddie's version of positivity was simple: trust your work when everybody else stops believing. Hold your identity when your image gets dragged. Stay solid when folks mistake your silence for weakness. That steady, quiet version of Eddie turned the same guy they once called the goat into one of the GOATs.

Flip It or Stay Stuck

I used to think reframing meant forcing yourself to be positive. Put on a smile through pain. Act like nothing bothered you.

But that's not it.

Reframing is slowing down long enough to ask if there's another way to see it. Something real you can stand on when nothing else feels steady.

I didn't get that in my playing days. My first major injury at OSU knocked me off track. Timing couldn't have been worse. I was rising up the depth chart, earning more carries, feeling the shot line up the way I'd imagined it since day one. Then outta nowhere, it was gone.

At first I sat in it. Mad. Embarrassed. Afraid the window was closing and I wouldn't get another shot. It felt like everything I'd built was slipping through my hands.

One of our coaches once showed me that old duck-rabbit illusion, how the same image flips depending on how you look at it. I didn't pay much attention then, but it stuck somewhere in my head.

When anger stopped getting me anywhere I came back to that idea. I was seeing a door slam instead of a new angle. So I flipped it. I started studying film harder and breaking down schemes. I learned the language of the line. I trained my eye to see blocks and angles the way I hadn't needed to before.

The work felt nothing like winning. It was survival. But that survival built a foundation I couldn't have made any other way.

I stopped chasing what I'd lost and focused on becoming a more complete player, smarter, tougher, more versatile. I turned what could have been a dead end into something that actually carried me forward.

Reframing didn't make the pain disappear. It kept the moment from owning me and put the choice back in my hands.

Overcoming Challenges to Positivity

Too Close to See It

I was dead wrong about Joey Galloway.

When you're young you live by unwritten rules: half street code, half insecurity. You decide who's worth your time based on vibe, how they talk, where they're from, who they remind you of. Joey was from the Valley. Different energy. Different pace. I boxed him out without giving him a shot.

I didn't hate him. I just didn't bother.

I stuck with the dudes who felt familiar and wrote off the rest. Meanwhile Joey was over there putting in work. Coming off an ACL injury, he kept showing up and producing. I wasn't even looking his way.

I missed all of it.

Yeah, I knew he was fast, but at Ohio State fast is a baseline. What I didn't see was the edge, the mentality that makes speed matter. We had 125 guys on that team, and I only paid attention to the ones who matched my narrow idea of what a "real one" looked like. Easy way to miss people. Easy way to miss growth. You think you're staying solid, but really you're playing small.

By senior year it hit me. Half jersey, helmet off after a TD, shit-talking like he owned the place. I remember thinking, Damn. I had this dude all wrong.

He became one of my closest friends. That bond could have started earlier if I hadn't been stuck on a picture in my head.

Positivity is letting people show you who they are before you assign them a role. If you only trust people who move like you, you cut yourself off from the strongest connections.

They Still Ain't Listening

John Cooper could recruit his ass off. He hit the road hard and stacked the roster with speed from Florida, Texas, Georgia and California. Ohio State was back in the national spotlight. It worked, until we had to play Michigan. Ha.

If you wanted a coach to put an arm around you, to talk you through the rough spots, Coop wasn't that guy. He ran the program like a business. His job was to coach the coaches. If you needed something, you went to your position coach. I never once sat with Coop in his office. Didn't bother me. My dad probably never sat down with the CEO of GM either.

Some guys struggled with the distance. They wanted more connection. They expected something Coop didn't offer. You don't get to pick your leader type.

Here's where it got real. After one rough practice I walked past Coop and he didn't even look. I wasn't expecting a hug, but damn, something. A nod. A look. A "keep going." Anything. I flashed back to recruiting visits when they told my dad they believed in me and promised to take care of me. Now, silence. For a second that bitter voice crept in: they don't care, so why should you?

I caught it. I didn't blow up. I didn't fake a smile. I said, "Alright. Cool. I see how it works." That could have pushed me off track. Instead it flipped me on.

Once I stopped waiting for something I wasn't going to get, I focused on what I could control. Effort. Attitude. Attention to detail. I made my reps count in practice and doubled down on film study. Simple moves: know the blitz, finish the run, clean the little things nobody thanks you for. The coach didn't matter. The choice did.

When teammates started venting about Coop, I cut it off. "Cool, but what are we doing to get ready for Saturday?" Small moves. They kept me out of the negativity trap.

Finding positivity is about where you put your attention. Guys who needed Coop to be something he wasn't handed their power away. I learned to look for opportunity, not excuses. Coop stayed Coop. The difference was how I handled it.

Same Start. Different Climb.

Freshman year, me and Zo moved as one. Where you saw him, you saw me. Inseparable. Big dude from Jersey, size 18 shoe, presence so heavy you felt him before you saw him. Alonzo Spellman was a force. Loud. Laughing. Unstoppable in every room he walked into. He'd joke through workouts, then move more weight than anybody. At 17, the most physically imposing player I'd ever seen. With Zo by my side, I stopped questioning whether I belonged, because I didn't have to carry that weight alone.

We weren't just teammates, we were brothers. Ate every meal together. Talked family, dreams, and what we'd do in the league one day. That kind of friendship where you don't even notice how close you've gotten until something pulls it apart.

We had the same dream. Same hunger. I thought we'd climb together.

Then life took us in different directions.

While I was redshirting, Zo was starting. Making his mark. By our junior year, he was a star: fans wearing his number, reporters chasing him all around. Meanwhile, I was still trying to prove I mattered. Still wondering if anybody noticed.

And slowly, the distance showed up.

He didn't do anything wrong. There was no fallout. No drama. Just fewer meals and shorter conversations. A hundred little signs we were drifting.

I told myself I was happy for him. And I was. But underneath all the support, I felt something I didn't want to admit...I'd been left behind.

That was my brother. Then one day, he wasn't.

That kind of loss is hard to name. There's nothing to fix and no one to blame. Just a space that used to feel full, and now doesn't.

First-round pick to the Bears. I'd see him on ESPN, living the life we used to joke over back in that apartment. And I'd sit there...just hollow.

These moments tested my core, and I didn't have time to dwell. I was still riding the COTA bus and heating up ramen noodles, trying to earn a spot while Zo was suiting up on Sundays.

Then, 1994. The universe spun the block. The Bears drafted me. All of a sudden, we were back in the same locker room, rocking the same uniform.

But we weren't those kids from the Towers anymore. Zo was a vet. I was a rookie. He was single. I was married. Our lives had stretched in different directions. But the bond? Still intact. Just worn in a different way.

Positivity had to carry me through these difficult stretches, when nothing else was working. I had to accept our new reality while moving forward on my own path. The old connection was gone, but something real still remained.

Some guys get there in three years. Some in five. How long it takes don't matter. What you do when you show up does.

Success Story: Barack Obama

I thought I understood what positivity meant, until I saw what it looked like when power and pressure collided with that kind of presence in one man.

They said he was too measured. Too calm. Not angry enough. But I saw it differently.

Barack Obama came out of Chicago with a tone most people didn't know how to read. He kept his foot on the ground while everyone else tried to fly.

People underestimated him because of that.

He wasn't loud enough for the activists or safe enough for the establishment. Nobody was clapping for that kind of control. But what made him dangerous was simple. He just did the work.

I felt that.

I've had rooms where I knew exactly what was being said without it ever leaving anyone's mouth. I've smiled through tension just to keep the moment from tipping over. Choked back responses that would've cost too much long-term.

Obama built trust in Chicago conversation by conversation. When he finally stood on a stage, people thought the power came from the speech. The power came from the years nobody paid attention to.

Real positivity looks like choosing patience when chaos would've felt better. Holding composure when frustration starts to burn. Because you're building something.

Even as president, people still wanted more fire. More anger. But he never gave in to that version of leadership. He didn't let pressure turn him into someone else. He made it through eight years without losing himself for a reason.

I wasn't in politics. But I know what it feels like to walk into rooms where you're not fully trusted. Knowing when to speak your truth is part of leadership.

Barack Obama wasn't the loudest in the room. But he was always the one playing the long game.

This was the positivity I've grown to respect.

Positivity Conclusion: Still Standing. Still Clear.

By my senior year at Ohio State, everything I'd fought for started to come together. Belief, patience, commitment, positivity, all of it built the hard way. When you approach difficulties with the right mindset, everything contributes to your growth instead of knocking you off course.

I had every reason to tap out along the way. Injuries. Depth chart games. Coaching changes. Doubt. I needed a mindset strong enough to hold all that weight, whether the world lightened up or not.

That season, things finally aligned. My mindset wasn't fragile anymore. I didn't need everything to go right. I knew how to make something out of what was left.

And when I walked off the field with Eddie after that Illinois loss, I knew exactly what he needed. I'd just lived it. You can't shield someone from pain. But you can walk with them through it. Just to remind him: he wasn't the failure they tried to pin on him.

Everyone remembers the Heisman...I remember the walk.

EMPowered to Act: Your Positivity Playbook

Flip the Frame

You're staring at a problem, but have you even tried flipping it yet? After my injury, I stopped grinding and started observing. I noticed patterns. I picked up things I used to miss. I leveled up my football IQ. That only happened because I stopped whining and started looking for value.

What's your version? Find what's testing you right now and ask: "How could this be helping me?" Then answer it. Not with fluff. With truth hiding under the pain.

Check the Room

The energy around you matters. It either keeps you steady or throws you off. Look around: who's feeding your mindset and who's draining it? You don't need to cut people off to see them clearly. Just start deciding where you spend your time and what you let into your head.

Move First, Feel Later

Don't wait for the "right mood." Waiting is the trap. Energy shows up after you move. When I was low, I started showing up with more energy on purpose: helping the young guys, being more vocal in drills. That behavior elevated my mindset.

Try that. One area you've been coasting or waiting on—step into it differently this week. Show up like it matters, even if your mood says otherwise.

The only permission needed is your own. And this positivity power... It's 100% in your control.

CHAPTER 5

ADAPTABILITY: WHO YOU WERE WON'T BE ENOUGH

ADAPTABILITY is the first cornerstone of our **PERFORMANCE** controls. It shows up when the plan falls apart and nobody's handing you a script. The ones who last don't wait for perfect. They move anyway.

The NFL will humble you fast. Draft day finally came. My name got called, fourth round to the Chicago Bears. Not the second round like I thought it should've been. But I wasn't thinking of any of that then. I was locked on proving I belonged, on chasing the dream I'd carried since I first touched a football.

Mini-camp. Bears facility. Fresh-cut grass. new gear., heavy air. Everything I'd worked for was right in front of me.

Then my position coach drops the same bomb I'd heard years ago: "We see you as a fullback."

It landed in my chest before I could brace. Breath tight. Hands cold. My head filled with the same scenes I'd fought to bury:

Ohio State, the whispers, the nights I tried to force my way back. History didn't just repeat. It came swinging. For a second I wasn't in mini-camp. I was back in that smaller room, invisible all over again.

Last time I heard those words, I didn't take the hit. I fought it. Pouted. Made excuses. Spent a whole season trying to force my way back into a role I thought I deserved. And it broke me. Worst year of my career. Life doesn't move on until you face the lesson it keeps putting in front of you.

This time, the situation hadn't changed. But I had.

Years of fighting for what I wanted kept me from becoming what I needed to be. What landed for me with adaptability was how much I had to release just to keep moving forward.

But letting go of that running back identity cut me to the core. I was that guy with the ball in his hands, making people miss, feeding off the roar of the crowd. Blocking instead of shining meant burying the kid in me who dreamed of the spotlight. It meant questioning who I even was if I wasn't that player anymore.

"Coach, I'll be the best fullback I can be for the Chicago Bears."

Saying it was easier than actually letting go. Every practice where I opened holes instead of running through them tested me. I'd catch myself watching the running backs, part judgement, part longing. But over time, I found new ways to measure success. Beyond yards. Beyond touchdowns. I started taking pride in chopping knees and stoning blitzers. I was rebuilding my identity play by play.

I was never defined by these titles or spots on a depth chart. I wasn't letting them shrink me. They made me a fullback. I made fullback, mine.

I wasn't defined by titles. Not by depth charts. Not by their labels. They thought they made me a fullback. Instead, I made fullback mine.

This wasn't for show. I locked in. Studied blocking like my job depended on it, turned pass protection into an obsession, and learned angles I'd never bothered to see.

We fight change because we confuse a name on the roster with who we are. We fight transitions, new positions, new jobs, new chapters, because we've mistaken what we do for who we are.

The toughest changes are never the physical or mental ones. It's shedding the story you've been telling yourself. I had to let go of "running back" before I could truly become something more versatile and valuable. Some people spend years fighting against their new reality, trying to get back to what feels familiar, while missing the growth waiting on the other side.

Adaptability changes you by force, then dares you to own the new shape. Deep down, we know that change is coming. It's whether you'll use it to become smaller or larger than before.

Six games in, I was the starting fullback. Two games later, I was the single back. By game ten, I wasn't leaving the field, short yardage, third downs, two-minute drills. The Chicago media started calling me the "Ultra-Back," the guy who could do it all because he wasn't stuck chasing what he thought he had to be.

The irony still gets me. I was better at the role I never wanted than the one I spent my whole life chasing.

All that time fighting change, I was really just fighting my own growth. If I'd embraced it earlier, maybe the second round wouldn't have been a dream. It would've been my reality.

But the NFL wasn't done teaching me. Four years with the Bears, then stops in Green Bay, Denver and New England.

Each move meant learning new systems. New playbooks. New ways of doing things.

Every time, it forced me to evolve or get left behind.

Standing still while everything else moves will get you cut. Your biggest breakthrough usually hides inside the change you're fighting against.

This chapter is the pause, just long enough to see change for what it is: the arena where your next evolution gets built.

That season forced me to stop performing and start becoming. I had to bend without breaking, and then figure out how to move in a whole new way.

Understanding Adaptability

Adaptability gets tossed around like it's just handling whatever gets thrown at you. But there's a big difference between accepting change because you have to and turning that change into something that works for you. I learned that difference the hard way, through each stop on my NFL journey.

Adaptability follows the same path as belief, patience, commitment, and positivity. It has levels to it. The deeper you go, the better you get at using change to push you forward instead of just trying not to let it break you.

Surface Adaptability: Not Bought In

Surface is where the average person stops, doing what they're told because they have to.

The first time I got moved to fullback in college, I fought it every step. I showed up. Did the drills. But inside, I was rejecting all of it. My body was present. My mind was somewhere else.

The OC pulled me aside after one of those half-hearted practices:

"Harris, you're giving me 50% of what you're capable of and that ain't good enough."

He wasn't wrong. I was physically there, but mentally I was still a running back being forced to play out of position. Every coaching point felt like a jab. Every rep carried resentment.

The danger with surface adaptability, it looks like change, but it's just compliance. You think you're "adjusting," but really, you're just surviving with a bruised ego.

This is how good players wash out. How people get left behind while convincing themselves they're doing enough.

From the outside, it shows up clearly: sluggish effort, up-and-down results, body language that screams I'll do it, but I hate this. From the inside, it feels like: I'm doing what I have to...without letting it touch who I really am.

But the cost is real. You miss the moments and the evolution. You end up as a watered-down version of your old self, clinging to what was, when you could've become something far more powerful.

Strategic Adaptability: Made It Mine

This is where change stops happening to you, and starts working for you.

When the Bears moved me to fullback, I didn't just accept it, I reimagined it. I looked at how my background as a running back could create mismatches and redefine the position.

I stopped asking how do I survive this? Instead, I was asking: how can I make this role something they've never seen before?

That changed everything. I started watching how linebackers reacted to different looks out of the backfield. I saw how my ability to read cutback lanes could help me create better blocking angles. I even used the threat of running the ball to mess with defenses.

Strategic adaptability repurposes your strengths and turns setbacks into leverage. You take control and design your response instead of just reacting to everything thrown your way.

Transformative Adaptability: Became the Change

The game changes when adaptability becomes identity.

Between the Bears, Packers, Broncos, and Patriots, I had to stop treating change like an obstacle, and start becoming someone who responded to chaos and moved like it was home.

Each system forced me to unlearn something old and absorb something new. By the end of my career, I had tools the rookie version of me couldn't even spell.

Green Bay meant adapting to Brett Favre's controlled chaos after years in Chicago's structured system. Denver forced me to learn zone-blocking after a lifetime of power football. New England? They spoke in code. Same play, three different names, depending on formation and situation.

At some point, the external changes stopped feeling external.

No longer was I playing out of position or a Bears guy in a Packers jersey. Now I was the guy who could make it happen wherever I suited up.

This unlocks the highest level of adaptability. When your identity is no longer what you do, it's how fast you grow when everything around you changes.

Adaptability at that level becomes both your shield and your sword. It protects you from getting left behind, and gives you the edge to carve a new lane forward.

Importance of Adaptability

Adaptability shows up when your identity gets tested under pressure.

It appears when your body can't move the way it used to. When your role completely changes and the playbook that worked last year becomes useless.

If you can't adapt? You break. If you can? You evolve.

Built for One Role, Forced Into Another

I trained for years to run, to make defenders miss and break tackles. Everything in me was wired for stiff arms and fighting for extra yards. Then one day... that job wasn't mine anymore.

My body spent eight years learning how to avoid defenders, now I had to seek out contact, initiate it, control it. My stance was too high. My base too narrow. I was trying to dodge at the last second, running back instincts, instead of delivering the blow. That muscle memory that served me for years? It worked against me in this new role.

Now I had to block instead of carry. Now my hands and feet had to retrain on the fly, under live fire. Against the best in the world.

I remember my first practice at fullback. Linebacker coming downhill. I braced like I was gonna sidestep. Instinct kicked in. And that instinct got me blown up.

The worst part? My years of muscle memory turned completely useless right in front of me.

Adaptability may ask for effort, but it demands humility, the willingness to suck at something you used to dominate.

It felt like the same thing a veteran carpenter goes through when he switches trades. Years of mastery in one space mean nothing in the next. All that skill turns into confusion. That's where I was standing.

Physical adaptability requires letting go of your old identity to become what's needed now.

Greatness Without the Credit.

I grew up wanting to be Walter Payton. But I had to become Matt Suhey.

As a fullback, I started doing things that helped others shine, without the crowd ever knowing it was me.

Clear the lane. Take the hit. Scoreboard lights up, and your name doesn't get called.

The first time it happened, I felt proud... and invisible.

I remember clearing the lane on a key block, touchdown. The crowd erupted. Cameras followed the guy who scored. I was still in the end zone when it hit me, my best plays might never get noticed.

Film on Monday. Running back gets praise for vision. My block that made it happen barely got a word.

I had to confront the truth. My version of success had to change or I was gonna crumble chasing recognition that wasn't coming.

Elite stopped being numbers. It became mastery.

That meant redefining the win. From "Did they see me?" to "Did I do the job right?"

Mental adaptability is what keeps you from burning out when the spotlight moves on. Because your value isn't in being seen. It's in what you bring to the room, even when nobody's watching.

Cultivating Adaptability

Every Room Got Rules

Success in a new environment starts before you say a word. It starts with listening. Watching. Seeing how the room really moves. Talent might get you in the door, but understanding people is what keeps you in the building.

Every locker room speaks its own language. Some quarterbacks want input. Others want silence. Some coaches micromanage. Others trust. You've got to figure out which room you're in.

When I joined the Packers after my years with the Bears, I walked in wearing a navy blue shirt. Seemed harmless. Somebody laughed and said, "You ain't in Chicago no more." I laughed too, but I got the point. The room had its own identity. If I wanted a place in it, I had to learn the rules.

Reading the room isn't passive. It's how you learn where trust lives and how influence really works. Same goes outside sports. A teacher moves schools after twenty years. She's still got wisdom. Still has value. But if she can't adjust her rhythm to that new hall, she gets left out.

As a rookie, I paid close attention. Who spoke in meetings? Who didn't, but still carried weight? Which guys kept showing up early when nobody told them to? That was how I started to separate titles from real leadership.

Eventually I saw it. The move wasn't about being noticed. It was about bringing value without needing the spotlight. The guys who didn't learn that? They were gone before anybody even remembered their name.

Shouldering A Different Load

When the Bears drafted the 1994 Heisman winner Rashaan Salaam after my rookie year, people expected drama. Two young backs in the same backfield. Carries on the line. Was there room for both?

But I looked at it differently. I shared everything I knew, our offense, reading NFL defenses, all of it. There was no strategic holding back. I had supreme confidence in myself and wasn't afraid of anyone taking "my spot." The way I saw it, we both had jobs to do and Salaam's skills could help elevate my game.

Then, on the first play of the first game of the season, I broke my collarbone. Just like that, I was out. I had to adapt mentally when I couldn't contribute physically, finding ways to add value that had nothing to do with speed or strength. I had a choice: fade into the background, or stay front and center and find a new lane.

I decided to stick close to the team, especially Salaam. During games, I'd watch the defense and relay small things between drives. "They're shifting when we motion." "That safety's creeping early." The stuff you can't always see when you're in it.

What started as support for him turned into survival for me. Because staying engaged kept me from falling apart. That injury humbled the hell out of me. I couldn't fix it by grinding harder. I had to sit in it. Adjust. Grow. Contribute in ways I hadn't before. Sometimes you gotta let growth get behind the wheel and put your ego in the back seat.

There Was No Welcome Mat

There's no manual for those first weeks in a locker room. You're good enough to be there, but you don't have a place yet. You're standing in the middle of it, trying to figure out rules nobody says out loud. With the Bears, talent got me through the door, but it didn't teach me how to move once I was inside. Even in meetings, there were boundaries you learned without anyone saying a word. Even something as simple as picking a seat on the plane had a pecking order. Vets had their space. Rookies knew better than to cross it.

I learned quick. Show up early. Watch more than you talk. Small things carried weight. The vets noticed the rookie who cleaned up without being told. Or the one who finished drills hard when nobody was looking. It wasn't flash. It was consistency. That's how you earned your way in.

One night after practice, a respected vet passed by my locker, paused briefly, and said just three words: "We see you." It wasn't much, but those words had weight. My quiet, consistent effort had finally registered. I didn't beg for it. I didn't fake it. I just kept showing up and letting the work do all the talking.

The hidden power of adaptability: You don't demand space. You earn it through the kind of effort that never chases attention but ends up speaking louder than words ever could.

Overcoming Challenges to Adaptability

Outgrown but Still Wearing It

I walked into Halas Hall with the same pride I carried at Ohio State, only quieter. I knew better than to act like I ran the room. Adaptability had to show up before they wrote me off. My ego sat down so survival could stand up. In the league, talent's a given. What they're watching is whether you can evolve.

The vets already had their names. The rookies were fighting every day just to stick. Nobody cared what you did in college. I saw guys brag on their old stats, acting like they were still campus stars. Most of them didn't last long. They couldn't stomach being unproven again.

I watched it all, knowing exactly what was coming. I didn't see myself in him, but I saw what could happen if you didn't adapt.

I'll never forget a film session early in camp. A rookie receiver wouldn't shut up, talking over coaches and correcting other guys. The room got quiet. Then a vet leaned back and said, "You do know this ain't college, right?" The room cracked up, but the point landed. Two weeks later, he was gone.

I saw it coming the whole time. He thought he was making a point. He was really just making it easy for them to cut him.

I learned quick to separate who I was from what I did. My value wasn't tied to a spot on the depth chart. Critiques stopped feeling personal once I saw them for what they were. I didn't have to agree with everything, but I listened. This level demanded it.

The old me had been useful. But holding onto him wasn't just pointless. It was dangerous.

Adaptability doesn't erase you. It forces you to grow into more than you were.

Success Was My Excuse

Success didn't make me lazy, it made me selective. Once I'd proven I could play, I got real particular with who I listened to. Especially coaches who never did what I did.

I didn't need somebody to pump me up. I didn't need rah-rah. I needed clarity. Realness. Somebody who'd actually been in it. But a lot of the time the loudest critiques came from guys who never played the position. Never felt the cut. Never saw the angle or the speed. They were guessing from a remote.

One coach kept pressing me, always on my reads. "Why didn't you cut there?" "What were you thinking?" I'd watch the tape and think, you don't even know what that cut feels like. You don't know the chaos.

I tuned him out. Stayed respectful on the outside, but I wasn't hearing a word. Success gave me cover. A track record. A reason not to listen to voices I didn't trust. I trusted the game. I trusted my instincts. But sometimes the game changes before your instincts do.

That was my mistake. I wanted to improve, but I wasn't open to learning new tools. Success gave me filters. It didn't give me results.

The game demands adjustment. Who you trust along the way is your business.

They Liked the Old Me Better

Every new team meant proving myself again. Could I adjust to the system? Would I fit the scheme? That doubt wasn't just in me. I could feel it in the way they looked.

External doubt cuts deepest when you're already questioning yourself. It's like trying to find your balance while someone tells you that you're about to fall.

With the Packers, I walked into my first practice carrying all the baggage of being "the Bears Ultra Back." Guys only knew me as a rival. I was learning a new playbook, new cadence, new tempo, but I caught myself pressing. Second-guessing things I used to do without thinking. Wondering if my game still fit.

Instead of getting defensive, I pulled aside a veteran linebacker who'd gone against me for years. I asked him, "When we played, what did you see? What do I need to clean up?" That question cut through the doubt. It showed I wasn't hanging onto the past. I was here to grow.

I didn't have to say "look at me" or prove others wrong. Adaptability is quiet. Not everyone notices when it happens, but you damn sure feel it when it's done.

Success Story: Toni Morrison

She was from Lorain too. But her path was nothing like mine. While I was adapting on the field, she was adapting through history. Toni Morrison embodied adaptability at the highest level. Born in a steel town that never expected brilliance from a Black girl, she gave them brilliance anyway.

Before the world called her legendary, she was Chloe Wofford. Raising kids. Working full-time. Stealing hours to write while the house was still dark. Something in her demanded to be written, even when nobody was listening.

She wasn't chasing acceptance. When publishers said Black stories wouldn't sell, she wrote them anyway. When critics called her books too complex, she made them do the work. She refused to water down the truth.

I've walked those same streets. Knowing she came from where I came from has always meant something. Lorain rolled out concrete, not red carpets. She built her foundation anyway.

Editor. Teacher. Author. Mother. Icon. She carried every role without breaking herself into pieces. She kept evolving because the work demanded it. The world kept turning, but she never got small to stay safe.

She guarded those stories with everything she had and made sure they lasted. *Beloved* ripped open wounds America wanted to bury. Her words got under your skin and stayed there.

She never waited for permission. She adapted on her own terms. She owned who she was and forced the world to meet her there.

She gave us more than books. She gave us proof. Proof that you could come from a small steel city with everything against you and still adapt without surrendering who you are.

Adaptability Conclusion: Had to Bend. Refused to Break.

There's a difference between knowing how to adapt and realizing what it unlocks. For me, that realization came under the lights against the defending champs.

My third year with the Bears, we opened against the Cowboys, the defending Super Bowl champs, on Monday Night Football. Fourth quarter, we're down four. Coach calls a play we'd been working on for weeks. They hand off a reverse to Curtis Conway while I slip out of the backfield after showing block. I get matched one-on-one with a linebacker, and C-Way drops a perfect pass only I can get.

That play proved what adaptability creates. My running back foundation gave me the moves to win that one-on-one. My fullback development created the deception that made it possible. The version of me that refused to evolve never would've experienced that moment.

Adaptability is rarely loud. Most of the time, it looks like showing up differently before anyone asks you to. It's learning a new system when the old one still works. It's crafting your role without making a speech about it. It's sacrificing comfort when something harder, but better, is asking for your attention.

The ones who last may struggle, but they don't panic when the room changes. They adjust and find a way without compromising who they are.

EMPowered to Act: Your Adaptability Advantage

Stop clinging to old tools - If the game has changed, stop playing it like it hasn't. Ask yourself: What habits, mindsets, or strategies worked back then, but are holding you back now?

Track where you resist - Adaptability usually shows up where you feel the most tension. That thing you keep fighting might be the exact thing you need to face. Write it down. Look it in the eye.

Move with intention - Adapting isn't weakness, it's strategy. What's one thing in your world right now that's changing? Instead of bracing against it, choose how you'll move through it.

Whatever changes you're facing right now, remember: They're happening to reveal you, not derail you. The best moments in your life, the touchdowns, the breakthroughs, the victories, often come from the changes you didn't ask for but learned to use.

And that choice? It's 100% in your control.

CHAPTER 6

CONSISTENCY: WHERE THE REAL ONES SEPARATE

CONSISTENCY is the second cornerstone of our **PERFORMANCE** controls. It's the quiet killer or the quiet proof, depending on how you show up when nobody's tracking the results.

New England Patriots, 2000. They brought me in to be the starting running back. Four backs on the roster. I was number one. Four quarterbacks too, including a skinny fourth-stringer named Tom Brady.

Brady didn't jump off the screen. No wow factor. No swagger you could sell to a crowd. But watching him closer told a different story. He showed up the same way every day. Same enthusiasm even if he only got one play in practice. Always prepared for whatever came his way. Carried himself like he already belonged before anybody gave him permission.

I noticed it. But I didn't think much of it at the time.

First preseason game, Hall of Fame Game, back in Ohio. I balled out. Home turf, hometown crowd. Felt unstoppable. Second preseason game, solid enough. Third game... fell off. Fourth game, just okay.

I convinced myself it didn't matter. Six years in the league should've been enough proof. Talent should've carried me.

Nobody said a word. But the silence told me everything.

The day before final cuts, we went golfing. Me, Drew Bledsoe, Eric Bjornson, and Brady. Everyone laughing, talking trash, like it was just another round. But under it all, we knew.

Brady was fighting for a seat. Maybe he didn't show it. But we felt it for him.

I pulled him aside. Tried to encourage him. "Hey man, you had a good camp. If it doesn't work here, some team will pick you up."

I meant it. At least, I thought I did.

The next morning, the call came. My agent's voice was tight: "They kept four quarterbacks." I was still half-asleep. "Wait, what? Four QBs? Why?" He didn't soften it. "They cut you. They kept Brady."

That call punched a hole straight through me. Stomach dropped. Heart racing. The roster spot. The starting job. Gone.

Cut for the fourth-stringer I thought I was helping. But he had already helped himself.

I could've blamed politics. Could've said they made the wrong call. But I knew better. They didn't pick potential over production. They picked consistency over flashes.

Brady didn't wait for the lights. He worked like it mattered when nobody cared. Same energy. Same mindset. Day after day after day.

Me? I showed flashes. The high moments were real. But the gaps in between cost me everything.

New England didn't care how talented you looked on your best day. They cared who you were on your worst.

When decision time came, they chose the player who never gave them pause. Brady treated even routine practices like they counted. They saw what was developing. It just hadn't been crowned yet.

When I got cut, nobody could've convinced me this was some life lesson. All I felt was the raw pain of losing everything I'd counted on.

But looking back, it was the most honest moment of my career.

Because the truth is simple: Flashes don't feed you.

Consistency does.

That's what this chapter is about. Understanding consistency at its core, and facing what it really costs when you don't have it.

Understanding Consistency

Consistency develops the same way character does, layer by layer, brick by brick. The deeper it roots, the less it needs sunshine to keep going.

Surface Consistency: Just Showing Up

People confuse showing up with effort. But showing up without giving a damn? That's just clocking in.

I saw it up close with Tom Brady when we were with the Patriots. I was pacing myself, holding back in practice like I had something to save. Brady treated every rep like it was the season.

He barely got reps. Three in a two-hour practice. But he attacked each one like it could change his future. No cameras. No crowd. Just a regular Tuesday and a rookie going full tilt.

I've seen plenty of guys whose energy rose and fell with the room. Coach walks by, they perk up. Coach leaves, back to half-speed.

Looking back, it's simple. If your standard depends on who's watching, it was never yours. Consistency starts when you stop performing and start owning it.

Strategic Consistency: The Hit in Tokyo

Fans remember the MVPs and the 2,000-yard season, but forget what built them.

Terrell Davis didn't blow up overnight. He built trust before he built stats. Before Denver knew him as their RB1, he was a sixth-rounder on special teams trying to survive camp.

Then came Tokyo.

Preseason game. Kickoff coverage. Some guys were coasting, some trying not to get hurt. TD? He punished a returner on special teams, full speed, no hesitation.

One hit. One rep. But it turned heads. The coaches looked up. Watched him closer. And that changed everything.

That play didn't make him famous. It made him believable.

Strategic consistency stacks trust, one decision at a time. You show up right on the days that don't 'count', and eventually, they all do.

TD didn't have the best workout numbers. He wasn't invited to the Combine. But he built something stronger than measurables...he built proof. And proof gets you invited to the Hall of Fame.

Transformative Consistency: The Film Don't Lie
Consistency tells the truth.

I learned that in New England. I had the paycheck of a starter, but I wasn't playing like one every week. My film told the story. Solid plays, sure, but too many disappearances in between. No separation. No dominance. Nothing that made their decision hard.

The Patriots cut me because they didn't have to guess. My inconsistency made their choice simple. That's how it works in the League. Teams don't gamble on flashes. They go with the player they can trust. Basic math. Simple economics.

Back then, I didn't see it. I thought past production was enough to carry me. But the truth is, being steady builds trust. And trust keeps you in the room longer than hype ever will. Trust gets built on scout team reps, the ones nobody celebrates but everybody remembers. The greatest players earned trust in practice because they brought the same standard every day.

I saw the same thing years later while working at a bank. There was a personal banker named Shawn. Not flashy. Not the manager. But everyone respected him. Shawn gave the same focused effort to every client. He followed through on promises. Returned calls when he said he would. No drama. No shortcuts. Clients started asking for him by name. Coworkers trusted him with the messy problems. Not because of one big moment, but because of how steady he was when nothing big was happening. He didn't need attention to stay consistent. He just did his job like it mattered.

Same rule applies everywhere. If people can't count on you, they won't call you. Spark guys flicker. Steady burns forever.

Importance of Consistency

Consistency doesn't let the environment decide who you are.

Results change. Circumstances shift. Roles move. Recognition fades. The only thing that matters is what doesn't.

Physical Challenges: Feel It Later

Football teaches you how to live with pain. Every snap's a collision. You stop expecting to feel good. You just learn to function through the hurt. You figure out the difference between pain that sidelines you and pain you can play through. You reset, get up, and go again.

I built consistency in that space. In Chicago, my routine never changed. Same warm-up. Same recovery, no matter how I felt. I kept my diet clean, even when my teammates were out eating trash. Some days I felt it, some days I didn't. But the standard never moved.

That carried into life after football. My first job was in mortgage lending. Nobody was hitting me anymore, but rejection came fast and hit just as hard. Doors slammed in my face five times a day. Promises to call back, never kept.

But I'd been trained for that. Take the hit, shake it off, keep moving. I knew how to operate inside pain without letting it change my effort.

Same thing you see in EMTs. They show up to scenes nobody wants to imagine. Blood on the street. Screams in the background. Fear everywhere. And they stay steady. They still feel it, but they don't flinch. They move with clarity inside chaos.

Consistency is refusing to let your outside dictate your inside.

Mental Challenges: I Ate. We Starved.

'97 should've been a high point. I was finally healthy. Finally starting. Putting up numbers. Touchdowns. Top-tier stats.

I was among the league leaders through the first half of the season. Three Buckeyes sat in the top ten in rushing: me, Eddie George, and Robert Smith. All of us carrying the ball for different teams but still representing the same school. Felt like everything I'd fought through was finally paying off, and I was doing it alongside my Ohio State brothers.

But every Monday, we came into the building after another loss. The team was falling apart. Coaches scrambling. Locker room flat. And I walked in carrying numbers that should've meant something. Only they didn't.

We lost our first seven games. At the halfway mark, we were 1–8. That kind of record messes with your head. Guys check out. The air gets heavy. You start wondering if anything you're doing even matters.

Nothing feels right when you're winning in a losing environment. You don't want to smile while the team bleeds. You don't want to flex stats when nobody else is eating. So you start asking: does any of this even matter?

I didn't feel like celebrating. I didn't want to talk about my numbers. What's the point of balling when the whole system's collapsing around you?

It's a different kind of mental challenge. Quiet. Heavy. You start to feel disconnected from your own success. Like maybe it doesn't count. Like maybe it's not even real.

But that year taught me something brutal and true:

If your consistency depends on results, you're not consistent. You're just convenient.

I had to show up the same, 1–8 or 8–1. Because once I let the record dictate my energy, I was already part of the collapse.

That stretch rewired me. I stopped asking what success was supposed to feel like. And I just kept showing up.

Professional Challenges: Still Great. Still Gone.

My rookie year, I was wide-eyed. Some of the dudes on that roster were straight-up legends, guys I'd grown up watching on TV. One of them, the OG, was a future Hall of Famer. Been in the league forever. Dominated his lane.

When it came time to do his thing, he was still elite. That part hadn't slipped. But the second they asked him to step outside that box, play the run, drop into coverage, you could see it. The effort dipped. The fire wasn't there. Coaches tried to look away, but they saw it too.

I got matched up against him in practice a few times. My job was to cut him low so we could get a quick pass off his edge. Nothing personal. Just part of the scheme. But he didn't take it that way. Every time, he barked on me, cursing, warning me to stay off his knees. I was trying to make the team. He was trying to protect what he'd already built.

Three games in, they cut him.

That shit had my eyes wide open. This wasn't some fringe player. This was a guy headed to Canton once he retired. One of the best to ever line up. And even HE got sent home because he wouldn't bring the same intensity to everything he was asked to do.

I finally got it: It's easy to bring your best when it's your favorite thing. It's easy when it plays to your strengths. But consistency is how you move when it doesn't. When the assignment feels beneath you. When the work feels thankless. When nobody's watching.

If the OG could get cut for picking his spots, anybody could.

Cultivating Consistency

Early Was My Edge.

Talent gets attention. But drawing a hard line and honoring it is what builds consistency. For me, that line was time.

I made a rule when I joined the Bears: I would always be early. Not just "on time," but early. Every meeting. Every Function. That wasn't the team rule. That was my rule.

And I kept it, even if no one else was watching.

Didn't matter if I was banged up or pissed off from a loss, I was still early. Because if my routine only held up when things were good, it wasn't a standard. It was a suggestion.

That discipline built trust. Coaches saw it. But more importantly, I noticed it. That rule I set on day one became part of who I was.

Consistency gets treated like some magical skill. It's not. It's what you repeat when no one's watching. It's the agreements you make with yourself when nobody's asking you to.

That standard becomes your anchor. And in a league where everything changes fast, you need something you can control.

Don't Let the Check Fool You

The league was my first real crash course in money, and the pressure that comes with it. Rookie deals might look big from the outside, but they go quick. And it's not always spent on cars or jewelry. A lot of it gets burned trying to take care of everybody. Family. Friends. People who were there for you when you had nothing.

That's where it stacks up fast.

From the jump, I tried to keep it simple. I didn't chase flash. Didn't try to play the part just to fit in. If I couldn't afford it, I didn't buy it. But even with all that discipline, I still got hit.

Early in my career, I trusted a former teammate, someone with the credentials, someone I respected, to help manage my money. He looked legit. But he mishandled a significant chunk of what I had. That loss didn't come from wild spending. It came from putting faith in the wrong hands.

That shook me. But it also woke me up. I had to start learning what I didn't know. I got smarter, more involved. Took control instead of outsourcing it. I didn't leave the league rich. But I left stable. And that gave me peace.

Financial consistency isn't sexy. It doesn't get glamorized, but it does give you options. And when the game's over, you're gonna want options you earned, not ones you're begging for.

Your Space. Your Rules.

I didn't need to get to Chicago to know how fast you could lose your edge. I'd already seen what bad habits did to good players, guys who had all the talent, but weren't on top of their game. I didn't want to be one of those stories.

I kept things tight. I knew what threw people off, and I wasn't giving it a chance to throw me. What I ate, how I slept, I was careful with what I allowed into my space, it all had to support what I was there to do.

No alcohol. No soda and I definitely wasn't smoking. I even stopped eating pork and red meat. Not just during the season, period. Some teammates thought it was extreme and maybe it was, But NOBODY ever questioned if I'd show up ready to work.

I treated my body and routines like a business. Kept the same lift schedule. Recovered the same way. Same pregame flow, always some pasta, always Wu-Tang, Mobb Deep, and DMX in my ears. It kept me centered while everything else was fluid.

The more I controlled my environment, the less it controlled me. No surprises. No off days. I cut out the noise so I could stay ready for whatever came next. Staying ready took discipline. Staying consistent took even more.

I Wrote My Story

Chicago's one of the biggest media markets in the country, and you learn real quick that what you say, and how you say it, shapes how people see you. I saw players wondering why stories didn't go their way after they'd blown off interviews. Some gave tired clichés. Or just avoided the media altogether.

I didn't operate like that.

I leaned into it with intention, nothing forced, nothing phony. I built relationships by learning reporters' names and showing interest in their families. No need to spin and no need to brown nose. Just being real and staying present was my approach, and that builds connection. That trust came back around, through doors I didn't have to force open.

When the stories were written, I had personality. I didn't sound like everybody else. That was the birth of "The Ultra-Back." People cared enough to pay attention because of more than just how I played.

Controlling your narrative means showing up consistently. Your presence and honesty make people see you the way you see yourself. It goes deeper than image.

The same thing applies off the field. People remember you when you're actually YOU. Passing out business cards or networking like it's a job interview won't get you there. People connect with authenticity. When they connect with you, they start rooting for you. Doors open from that connection.

Overcoming Challenges to Consistency

Not Their Guy Anymore

I got to Green Bay during training camp. Still coming back from the broken ankle. Not 100%. Still learning the system. But in this league, none of that matters once the season starts. You're either producing or you're not.

My position coach, Harry Sydney, had played six years in the league and won two Super Bowls, as a running back. He'd lived the experience. He didn't coach us like kids. We were grown ass men, and he treated us that way. I came in during the fire, so we had no time to bond. Just daps and get to work. I respected that. No hype, just straight up feedback.

I started off making plays and earning trust. But then I did something I'd never been known for, I fumbled. Not once. Not twice. Three weeks straight. A running back's first job is to protect the ball. When you can't do that, nothing else matters. I could feel something change.

He didn't stop coaching me. But the energy behind the corrections changed. The urgency faded. He'd move on quicker. And when another back came in and started making plays, that gap widened even more.

At first, I brushed it off. Maybe he was giving me space to figure it out. But deep down I knew better. The truth sat heavy: he'd started investing in someone else. And in this business, coaches rarely say it out loud. They just start saying less.

It works this way: fewer reps, less correction. The belief gets transferred without a word.

You feel it without anyone having to say a word. And once it happens, your rhythm's gone. You start pressing. Trying to make something happen. Hoping one big play changes the story.

But at that point...it's already too late.

Coaches don't always bench you with words.

Sometimes, they just stop looking your way.

Winning Made Me Careful

My mistake with the Patriots started right after the first preseason game. Monday Night Football. Against the 49ers. I ran hard. Gave work. For the first time in a year and a half, I felt like myself again.

It was my first real game in over a year. I'd sat out all of '99, still trying to bounce back from the broken ankle in '97. Camp had given me contact, but this was different, these were live bullets. Bright lights. Real pressure.

Some of the guys had seen me run before. Others weren't sure if I still had it. Running backs don't get long lifespans in this league. Year three is when most start slipping. I knew that. So, I showed up like I had something to prove.

And I proved it. But instead of using that game as fuel, I exhaled. Walked into the building the next day thinking, I'm back. Just make it to the season.

What I didn't realize was that I'd already changed. Mentally. I wasn't attacking anymore. I was protecting. I wasn't playing to dominate, I was trying not to get hurt. That mindset showed up fast.

Especially because New England wasn't just another stop. It was the only shot I had left. The season before, nobody called. The year before that, I flamed out in Green Bay, still hurt, still trying to find my legs. Booed by fans who once booed me for bullying their team. I was stuck. No team. No clear plan. I spent that whole year back in Columbus, training in silence, hoping for a call.

When the Patriots finally reached out, I didn't just see a roster spot. I saw a shot at saving my career.

So yeah, I wanted it bad. But I wanted it so bad... I lost the edge that made me dangerous.

The staff saw it. I gave them moments. But the spaces in between told a louder story. One hesitant step turns into two. One lazy rep becomes a pattern. Before long, I wasn't someone they could trust to show up the same way, every day.

Same thing happens in relationships. You start out strong with calls, effort, attention. Then you feel secure, and the urgency fades. You protect the comfort and stop reaching. And that slow pullback? It's not always laziness. A lot of times, it's fear.

Looking back, all those injury thoughts were in my head, I was just scared to break again. But fear doesn't show up on tape. All they saw was hesitation.

And in this league? Hesitation gets you cut.

The coaches didn't care why it was happening. They needed certainty. And results always speak louder than reasons.

No Eyes on Me

Tony Carter came into my rookie class undrafted. He arrived with a name on a long-ass roster and nothing more, no expectations or guarantees. Every day, he would grind. He played scout-team linebacker and served as a tackling dummy, taking whatever reps he could get. Most eyes weren't on him, but he still showed up like he had something to prove.

And it stuck with me.

Tony gave the same effort whether coaches were watching or not. You'd always see guys coast through scout team reps and only be aggressive when the head coach was nearby, not Cart, his switch stayed on. He had a standard that didn't care who was watching, or whether anyone clapped.

He didn't make the 53-man roster. But the team kept him on the practice squad. Same mindset. Same work ethic. When an injury opened up a spot, they didn't go searching. They elevated Tony. Eventually, he became a starter and played nine years in the league. That doesn't happen by luck. Consistency builds that in the shadows.

Kevin Hart's comedy career started the same way. No sold-out arenas. No blockbuster movies. Just empty rooms and brutal sets. He bombed more than he succeeded early on, but he kept showing up. Rewriting. Sharpening. Delivering with the same fire whether it was five people or five hundred.

Keep showing up, when it feels like no one cares if you do or don't.

Tony Carter kept grinding whether coaches noticed or not. When opportunity finally came, his readiness revealed what had been true all along. His standard was set by him...no one else.

And nobody embodies that better than Jay-Z.

Success Story: Jay-Z

Jay-Z didn't come in with the machine behind him. No record deal. No label push. Just rejection after rejection. That's why he built his own lane.

He pressed his own records. Hustled out of car trunks. Partnered with Dame and Biggs to create something real because nobody else believed in it.

That always hit me about Jay. He didn't start flashy, he started focused. Same standard, every time. Kept showing up like the world just hadn't caught up to what he already knew was coming.

He dropped *Reasonable Doubt* and it barely made noise at first. But he stayed at it. *In My Lifetime, Vol. 2, Blueprint, Black Album.* No gimmicks. No identity swaps. Just growth, album to album, deal to deal. Never rushing, never faking the image. Just showing up, track after track, move after move, whether the buzz was there or not.

I was in my third year with the Bears when *Reasonable Doubt* dropped. Jay was building his own lane. His mindset mirrored what I was learning, showing up every day, when it felt thankless, when it looked like no one was paying attention. He was skilled and intentional. That album felt like the truth I needed to hear.

I respect the droughts between the drops more than the shine. The times nobody's checking for you, and you stay consistent anyway.

I felt that in my own life. When the spotlight dims, but the work's still there. When the buzz fades but the bar stays high.

Jay moved like a man with receipts the world hadn't read yet. He was executing a blueprint. He just stayed in the work long enough to see it turn into something bigger than music.

He built methodically, phase by phase, brick by brick. His standards stayed high even through "Reasonable Doubt."

Consistency Conclusion: Consistency Never Lies

My Patriots story taught me a brutal lesson: intentions mean nothing compared to actions. I thought I was being smart by holding back, saving myself for the regular season. Meanwhile, Brady, buried as QB4, attacked every practice, meeting, and film session like a starter. The coaches didn't see my strategy. They saw my inconsistency. And they chose his character over my potential.

The spotlight lies. It shows the TD celebration but skips the system behind it. It shows the championship moment but ignores the work that made it possible.

What separates championship teams from talented rosters? What turns potential into results? The gap almost always comes down to consistency. And over time, consistency becomes character.

It starts with showing up. No fanfare, no special circumstances, just being there. And over time, it stops feeling like effort. It gave me a way to chase the love I didn't know how to name.

Sometimes consistency feels boring. Repetitive. Like a chore. But for me? It was freedom. You stop guessing how you'll show up, and so does everyone else. The effort it used to take becomes the standard. Your character handles what used to take willpower.

Each controllable builds on the others, but consistency might be the one that reveals the most. Belief gave me a foundation. Patience gave it breathing room. Commitment locked me in. Positivity gave me perspective. Adaptability helped me stay loose.

But consistency? That one never let me lie to myself.

Own that truth: consistency reveals everything. Especially when things stop making sense. Shortcuts start to feel earned. And your character either shows up or disappears.

And that character? It's 100% in your control.

EMPowered to Act: Your Consistency Code

Set the standard—and keep it. Pick one thing you'll do regardless of how you feel. Be early. Finish strong. Do it right the first time. Then don't waver. No matter the mood. No matter the day.

Track what no one sees. Forget applause. Consistency lives in the small, thankless stuff. What's one thing you do daily that proves you're still locked in, even when nobody's looking?

Catch yourself slipping. You won't see it all at once. It fades in small ways until one day you're way off track and don't even know how it happened. Where are you letting things slip? Don't wait for someone to point it out. Handle it now.

CHAPTER 7

RESILIENCE: BUILT THROUGH THE HITS

RESILIENCE is the third cornerstone of our **PERFORMANCE** controls. It's what lives in that space between broken and rebuilt, where you find out what you're really made of.

People ask me all the time: "What was the hardest hit you ever took?"

They expect names, Ray Lewis. Junior Seau.

Big collisions. "Top Ten Plays."

Truth is, my hardest hit didn't come from a linebacker.

It came standing in the parking lot outside my apartment in Foxborough.

Watching my wife, my mother-in-law, and my two youngest kids pull in after an 800-mile drive from Ohio.

They were smiling. Tired, but smiling.

Ready for a new chapter we couldn't wait to start.

And I had to tell them the chapter had already ended before they even unpacked the car.

I can still see it, their faces through the window. Hope. Pride. Exhaustion from the road. And me standing there, trying to swallow the lump in my throat before they opened the door.

My heart was beating so fast it felt like I was having a heart attack.

My mind racing, already making excuses, already searching for a way to soften the blow that couldn't be softened.

How do you say it?

How do you look your family in the eye and tell them the dream they just sacrificed for is already dead?

They deserved better. And all I had was the truth. I didn't make the team.

The shame, the embarrassment, every emotion you can name bubbling up inside me.

More painful than any hit I ever took on a field.

Football was my identity.

It was the thing that gave structure to a life that didn't always have it.

The thing that made me feel enough when nothing else could.

Losing a paycheck couldn't compare to losing the piece of myself I'd spent my whole life building.

Losing a roster spot hurts. Losing your identity breaks you in ways you don't have words for.

I'd adapted to new roles before. New teams meant new playbooks in new cities. That kind of change forces you to adjust your tools.

But this was more than a role shift. This was a soul hit.

When you lose the job and the whole frame you built your life around, adaptability stops being enough. Now it's rebuilding with no blueprint. This is where resilience steps in. Adaptability helps you bend. Resilience decides if you break.

Everybody faces some version of that moment, maybe it's a job ending before you're ready, a relationship collapsing, or a dream falling apart. The floor drops, and you're in free fall.

What separates the ones who rebuild from the ones who stay broken is never talent or luck, but the willingness to face the loss without letting it define you. To sit in both the pain and the possibility.

Resilience doesn't come with a trophy. It comes with scar tissue. It's sitting in that silence long enough to hear what it's trying to teach you.

I didn't understand how much football meant, until it was gone. It was my first love. My best friend. It was how I survived.

From the first time I lined up for that orange #20 jersey back in Lorain, football gave me something I didn't know how to ask for. The game gave me structure when life felt chaotic. It gave approval when home felt cold. It gave me a way to chase the love I didn't know how to talk through.

Every workout, every drill, every practice, every challenge, it was more than just a job.

It was the proof I'd been chasing my whole life. Something I could point to and say, "See? I AM worthy." Even if my father couldn't say the words.

I spent years outrunning the silence. Burying pain under helmets and pads. Turning anger into motivation.

When the game leaves you, the demons don't pack up with it.

They stay.

And now they've got nothing standing between them and you.

Guys cope in different ways after the game ends. The drinking starts to fill those empty spaces. Others lose themselves in meaningless relationships. Many create busy work disguised as purpose, anything to keep from sitting still with the silence.

Me?

I tried to power through it the same way I always had.

But I couldn't muscle through depression.

I couldn't double down on a dream that was gone.

Resilience is standing there in the aftermath, figuring out who the hell you are when there's nothing left to prop you up.

It's facing the real you.

The scared, unsure version that the game always saved you from.

And choosing to build anyway.

This chapter acknowledges the real pain, faces it head-on, and rebuilds from the ashes.

Understanding Resilience

You don't really understand resilience until you've had to live it.

And somehow, standing in Massachusetts, the birthplace of independence, was where I had to fight for my own. Watching my family walk into a future I hadn't planned for...that was the test of all tests.

There's no shortcut to resilience. It builds in layers. The more pressure you face, the more you find out what you're really made of.

Surface Resilience: Resilient on Paper

We love the highlight version of resilience, the comeback video, or the bounce-back story that makes everything look clean.

But real life doesn't work like that.

Surface resilience moves fast but skips the truth. It celebrates returning to normal without ever asking if normal was even good for you.

I saw it in teammates who masked injuries to stay on the field. They "pushed through," but ended up with permanent damage. Short-term toughness. Long-term cost.

That kind of resilience looks brave. But it's a trap.

You endure without evolving. Survive without learning. Your strength starts hiding your pain, and nobody, including you, stops to check if you're breaking under it.

Surface resilience rushes you back to who you were, even when what you need is something new.

Strategic Resilience: The Storm Didn't Pass

The next level is where the work gets honest.

I had to stop surviving the Storm and start recognizing I was the one creating it. I wasn't being ambushed by life. It was me just repeating patterns I never examined.

When football ended, the truth landed hard: I had built my entire identity on something temporary. And when it collapsed, so did I.

I thought I could outrun the silence. Stay busy and prove myself into feeling whole. But all it did was delay the crash.

Strategic resilience forced me to finally listen to myself. Why did certain days pull me under? What actually gave me a sense of worth beyond being an ex-athlete?

The setbacks started talking back. These were not whispers, they sounded like James Earl Jones with information. It wasn't pretty. But it was real.

Strategic resilience pulls meaning from the breakdown. Look beyond how fast you bounce back. The real question is: what are you bouncing back into?

Transformative Resilience: Rebuilt in Gold

Strength shows itself when you stop surviving and actually start becoming someone new.

I once heard of Kintsugi, this Japanese art where broken pottery gets filled with gold. It made too much sense to ignore. The cracks become the story. The broken parts get honored. That shit resonated.

That's transformative resilience. The scars become highlighted rather than hidden. Pain transforms instead of being denied. That hit hard. Because after football, I couldn't go back. I had to become something I hadn't yet imagined. The skills I developed as an athlete, discipline, teamwork, preparation, performance under pressure, weren't just for football. They were tools for life. But I didn't really own them until I stopped defining myself by what I had lost. The transformation happened gradually. I felt it when I could talk to people and not feel the need to change the subject when football was brought up. I started applying the same focus that read defenses to reading credit reports and appraisals.

Rejection couldn't take me out. I'd already come back from worse.

I used to look at my scars and see damage. Now I see them for what they really are, evidence that I kept going.

Importance of Resilience

Resilience goes deeper than toughness. It's what you rebuild when everything collapses, not how much you can take. It's becoming someone new through the remains, not just bouncing back.

Physical Challenges: No Pads for This

Football taught me how to take hits. I knew the difference between soreness and danger. I could reset fast, absorb the hit and shake it off. There was no need to dwell on it, because the next hit was on the way. But then I stepped into the business world. And the hits came in silence.

The hits came different now, cold shoulders and ignored emails. Phone calls that never came back felt like a blindsided hit that I didn't prepare for.

I'd sit in meetings with realtors and insurance guys, smiling, talking, and the second it got real? Gone. Vanished. Like the conversation had never happened.

It stung in a different way. Because I wasn't trained for this kind of hit.

Football pain had rules. These hits didn't.

There was no sideline to run back to or a coach to help me see the full picture. No huddle to regroup. Just me, sitting in the car afterward, staring at the dashboard, trying not to take it personal.

~~So~~ From there, I built my own reset. Every time a "no" came, I ran the meeting back in my head. What could I control? What did I miss? And then I'd say to myself: One play. Next one's coming.

That ritual became my helmet. My pads. My huddle.

It still stung. But I stopped letting it rewrite who I was.

Resilience lives in the getting back up, when your knees are shaking and every voice in your head is screaming to stay down. When you're not sure you can take another hit. You get up anyway.

Mental Challenges: Nobody Saw the Limp

After New England cut me, I spiraled. I didn't realize how much losing my job would affect losing my identity. The field was gone. The crowd, the structure, the brotherhood. All of it.

I hid it well, because that's what we're taught to do. Act okay and keep it moving. Just pretend everything's fine.

But the truth? I was waking up with no reason to get out of bed. I always wanted to be Walter Payton the football player. Now I was...what? A has been? A washed-up pro?

In football, the physical pain eventually fades. The mental pain? That shit has its own legs.

Broadcasting should've felt like a win. Instead, it was torture. I wasn't watching the game, I was watching the life I'd lost. Breaking down players who'd taken my spot. Analyzing a sport I should've still been playing. Every segment felt like the bitter vet taking knocks at the young guys, because they weren't doing it the way I would've done it.

The limp was real, but it was invisible.

Resilience showed itself as tiny anchors, therapy and coaching my kids, while studying sports that didn't cut as close. All helped with getting further away from the angry cynical guy and moving toward a healthier transition. Each one showed me I could still contribute something valuable, even without football.

Eventually, I stopped chasing my old life. And started building something out of what was left standing.

Professional Challenges: Doors Kept Closing

Professionally, I've been humbled. More than once.

Mortgage lending was never in my plan. I wasn't a big numbers guy and I lightweight hated math... But there I was, suit and tie, knocking on doors that didn't open.

Some realtors already had their 'person'. Insurance guys would string me along, making sports small talk, then ghost. Meetings would start out promising, then vanish the second business got real. People smiled while moonwalking through the side door.

I'd get strung along. Brushed off. And yeah, it messed with me. I started questioning whether I even belonged in the room. I knew how to take a hit on the field. But learning to take one in a sweater vest? That was new.

There was no sideline to jog to. No coach to call the next play. Just me and the quiet.

I had to build my own reset.

My car became my locker room. My steering wheel, my film session. After every failed meeting, I'd sit and ask: What did I miss? What can I change?

Not to punish myself, just to learn.

I still heard "no" a lot. But I quit hearing "no" as "you're not enough."

Resilience meant staying in the game, even when the field wasn't mine. Even when the rules weren't familiar. I kept showing up. Because I knew how to operate through pain. And I wasn't done proving I could.

Relational Challenges: The Basement

The basement wasn't just a place. It was rock bottom.

After the separation, I stayed in my buddy's basement, on an air mattress, surrounded by the clack from the dryer and my thoughts. The family laughter upstairs made the silence around me even louder. It was failure echoing in every corner of those cold, dusty walls.

She'd been with me through all of it. From college to the NFL and through real life. Losing that kind of history made any and every football loss feel small. I had to sit with what I'd done and what I hadn't done. No sugarcoating. Just pain for my role in unraveling my family.

At times the failure was loud, but it was usually quiet. Heavy and unrelenting. Dare I say, suffocating.

I'd lost more than a marriage. I'd lost who I thought I was. No plan B and no playbook. Just the moment. Just me.

Two of my kids were already grown. My youngest was still finishing high school. There was no blueprint for this next chapter. All I knew was I had to keep showing up, even when I didn't know who I was showing up as.

I wanted to keep myself busy by trying to fix everything, but the real work was staying present. Picking up the phone. Being honest with my kids, even when I didn't have answers.

I was flawed and broken, but they didn't need me to be perfect. I was just trying to be present. Someone they could count on through the difficult time, even if I was still rebuilding from the floor up.

That's what resilience looked like for me. There was no bounce back, this was a slow climb and a silent rebuild. The decision to be there, even while I was falling apart.

Cultivating Resilience

It Was Me. It Was Always Me.

Resilience starts with brutal honesty. After football, I kept waiting for things to "get back to normal." I expected another team to call with an offer. I thought my identity would somehow put itself back together. I wasted months waiting on something I already knew deep down wasn't coming.

I remember sitting on the couch, watching highlights of guys I knew I could outplay. Still telling myself a call was coming. Still chasing ghosts instead of building a future. I kept watching, hoping I'd see something that made me feel connected. Instead, I saw the truth: the league had moved on. And I hadn't.

Holding on to the tiniest hope that my agent would call and say... "you ready?" The truth finally hit me, I was living in a fantasy instead of preparing for my actual future. No dramatic moment marked the transition. Just a quiet realization that I needed to move forward.

Real resilience demands seeing your situation clearly. Not through the lens of what you wish was happening or what you think should be happening, but what's actually in front of you. The NFL didn't call. My football career was over. I struggled to know who I was without the game. Accepting these facts wasn't giving up. It was the first step toward building something new.

Brick by Brick

Football gave me structure. Everything was laid out: OTAs, team meetings, game plans, and routines. Then it all ended with silence. No schedule. No more check-ins. Just me staring at a blank calendar trying to figure out what the hell to do next.

I had to build my own anchors. Something to hold me down when nothing else would.

I got up at 5am every morning because I needed something steady. Some mornings I killed the weights and cardio, and others just sauna and flexibility. This routine gave the day shape.

Tuesdays used to mean game checks. Now they were check-ins. I'd read about athletes who figured out life after the game, Junior Bridgeman, Magic Johnson. I wasn't trying to copy them. I just needed proof it was possible to build something new.

On Wednesdays, I coached my son's baseball team. This was about time with my little man. Passing something on. Those kids needed someone to show up. And truth is, so did I.

Sundays hit hardest. Game days. I'd have to go for a walk. Just to let the pain breathe without an audience.

Those anchors of morning discipline, Tuesday reflection, Wednesday coaching, and Sunday walks were proof that I could still move, even with no scoreboard.

Finding New Goalposts

What I love about football is you always know where you stand. The scoreboard doesn't lie. Your stats tell a story that can't be disputed. You know right away if you're valuable or just taking up space on the roster.

When I left that world, I struggled to figure out what success even looked like anymore. The old measuring sticks disappeared, and I had no new ones to replace them.

Eventually I found different ways to gauge my progress. Being present for my kids mattered more than any stats sheet. Making an impact on someone's day counted as a win. Helping my son through a tough baseball practice or showing up to my daughter's track meet just to make sure she knew I was there. While still making time to talk a former teammate off the edge when life was beating him down. Doing something uncomfortable, especially the stuff I used to avoid, became its own kind of win. These weren't organized into some fancy system. No spreadsheets. No titles. Just little reminders that I was still showing up.

The real wins became smaller and quieter: showing up fully, owning my missteps, and facing what I used to avoid. That was the new scoreboard.

The Mask Was Too Heavy

Isolation kills resilience. After football, people would ask how I was doing?

I'd always say, "I'm good," nod my head, and change the subject. I didn't have the words, or maybe I just didn't feel like I was allowed to say them. I'm from the '70s, where men were taught to be strong and never show vulnerability, because that meant weakness. I rarely let people see my struggles. I'd been the strong one for so long that I didn't know if there was space to be anything else. If I was hurting, I kept it to myself. I've always handled it that way.

But the weight started showing up in other ways. The days were blah. Heavy in a way I couldn't explain, but never loud enough to make me stop. I was worn out all the time. Snapping at people for no reason. Couldn't sleep. Didn't want to leave the house. I'd still show up when I had to, still play the part. But inside, I felt like I was disappearing.

I had people close to me who noticed. A few tried to pull me aside. But how do you explain that you're struggling when your whole identity was built on holding it together? I didn't even know what I needed. I just knew I didn't want to look weak.

Then I ended up at this event for former players. No stage, just a group of guys sitting in a circle, chopping it up. One by one, they started sharing their transition. Just telling the truth, how hard it's been. Real stories. No superhero spin. Some talked about feeling forgotten. Never feeling safe enough to say things out loud. The league chewed them up and moved on, and now they were owning their truth.

And for the first time in a long time, I didn't feel crazy. Or alone.

I didn't say much that night. But I heard enough to feel like I could finally breathe. Because I knew I wasn't the only one carrying it.

The pain was the pain. But the silence, made the mask feel like a jail.

Overcoming Challenges to Resilience

Built on Bruises

Football ending left a hole I didn't know how to fill. My body had the scars and bruises to show, but the pain wasn't just physical. It reminded me I'd been in it. That I was one of the best in the world...and I wanted to hold onto that.

People love to say "move on" like it's a light switch. Like I hadn't already tried. The league moves forward without blinking. You're the one left staring at the wall, waking up at the same time every morning with nowhere to be.

I missed the structure of the game. There was always competition and a sense of urgency. And I loved the way pain had purpose.

Without it, the days just...dragged. No meetings to keep you on schedule and no brotherhood to be accountable to. Never thought I'd miss that moment right before a coach rewinds the film, asking why the hell I'm going the wrong way. You start questioning if your shine still counts if nobody cares anymore.

I wasn't sure how to exist without it. That weight, that pressure, it shaped everything. Without it, I didn't feel grounded. I felt too free.

Some mornings I'd wake up and, for a split second, forget it was over. Then it would hit me. It felt like a bad dream. That second before the truth landed stung the most.

I held onto the pain because it was the last thing that still felt like mine. Letting go felt like saying none of it mattered. Like the whole thing had just passed through me.

I lost the thing that gave me competition, brotherhood, love, validation, and money. That held me down.

Nothing else felt heavy enough to hold me. That was the hardest part.

The Steps Didn't Make Sense

I kept expecting healing to arrive on time, but life rarely happens that way. It showed up crooked. Unpredictable. I'd have a good week, then spiral over something small. A song. A highlight. A smell that took me back. I hated that. I wanted the growth to feel clean. Like I could get it done and never have to look back. But progress doesn't work like that.

I kept telling people I was fine, like saying it enough times would make it true. But behind closed doors, it was different. Some days, I believed it. Other days, I felt like I hadn't moved an inch. I was still hoping for a phone call that wasn't coming. Still replaying mistakes I couldn't change. Still waking up wondering if anything would ever feel normal again.

I didn't get it at the time. But the back-and-forth, that was the work. Every time I slipped, I had to make the decision to get back up again. The muscle got built right there. The stuff I tried to ignore just kept showing up.

The breakdown's gonna come. What saves you is remembering what you've already made it through.

Still Me...But Not Really

I kept measuring life after football against everything the game gave me, and nothing measured up. Broadcasting gave me a seat close to the action, but it didn't feel like being in it. Office small talk couldn't hold a candle to locker room trash talk. And trying to build new friendships without sweat, blood, and banter? Damn near impossible. That constant comparison kept stealing whatever peace I was trying to build.

What finally helped was noticing different wins. Broadcasting gave me a chance to tell stories that helped fans see the game in a way they hadn't before. The new relationships weren't built on shared suffering, but they matched where I was headed, and maybe who I'd been all along, before football gave me armor.

This kind of adjustment doesn't happen once. It loops back. You think you've let go, and then something drags it back up. But the more you face it, the less it owns you. The game stopped being the only place I saw value, and the loss stopped being the only thing I felt.

Success Story: Maya Angelou

Before the books. Before the fame. Maya Angelou was silent.

At eight years old, after being sexually abused by her mother's boyfriend, she testified in court. The man was released...then murdered, probably by her uncles. Ms. Angelou blamed herself. Thought her words had killed him. Thought speaking could destroy.

That's when she stopped.

No sounds. No voice, for almost five years.

That silence came from trauma. The kind that folds people in half and keeps them there.

What's wild is the very thing that saved her later, her voice, was the part of herself she feared most. The tension in that still resonates with me.

She could've stayed quiet. Could've disappeared into that pain. But slowly, she started reclaiming what the world told her to shut down.

Books helped. A teacher pushed her. Gave her permission to speak. And eventually, she did.

Her whole life was resistance. Not loud resistance, steady resistance. Through racism. Through exile. Through single motherhood. Through judgment. Through betrayal. She kept writing. Kept responding. Kept showing up.

Ms. Angelou put her pain on the page. Gave it shape. Gave it rhythm. And in doing that, she gave it power, without letting it control her.

Her words still live, because they weren't written from the top of the mountain. They came from the bottom. And she didn't clean them up for anybody.

She once wrote:

"You may encounter many defeats, but you must not be defeated... so you can know who you are, what you can rise from, and how you can still come out of it."

That wisdom came from living through it.

Ms. Angelou didn't get her voice back all at once. She fought for it. Line by line. Page by page.

She carried the weight of that silence for years, but she didn't let it define her. She didn't erase the past. She wrote through it.

Every sentence was a reclaiming. Every poem, a reminder that survival isn't quiet.

She showed the world that your response can be louder than what tried to silence you.

Resilience Conclusion: Built in the Hurt

The Patriots cut me deep, but it forced a question I'd dodged for years: Who am I when the cheering stops?

Football was my shield. Behind the uniform, I could hide from childhood pain, from questions I never wanted to answer, from a silence I didn't want to hear. But once that shield dropped, I stood exposed, to the world and to myself. I couldn't hide behind performance anymore. Couldn't bury the pain with crowd noise or jersey pride.

Some days I didn't feel strong. I didn't feel anything. But I kept getting up. I ate. I moved. I stayed in motion. Because I didn't know what would happen if I stopped.

This chapter held the raw stuff, depression, identity loss, silence, and the slow climb back. Pain broke me open and revealed what was inside.

The path through pain is messy. I clung to the ghost of football long after it left. Measured everything against moments I'd never get back.

And for every step forward, there were stumbles I couldn't fake my way through.

The version of me that walked through the fire isn't the same one that went in, and that's the whole point.

EMPowered to Act: Your Resilience Toolkit

Reclaim the moments you didn't fold - Think of a time you got knocked down and kept going. What did you lean on? What got you through? That wasn't luck. That was something real.

Sometimes you need to slow down just to keep going - Resilience doesn't mean grinding nonstop. It's knowing when to pause, and when that pause turns into hiding. Take the break, but don't lose the mission.

Let the scar teach you - The pain happened. Now what? Find the lesson. Apply it forward. Your scars aren't the headline. But they better show up in the story.

When the bottom drops, when the titles fade, and nothing feels familiar, your real self steps forward. Not the role. Not the jersey. Just you. And that discovery? It's 100% in your control.

CHAPTER 8

EFFORT: PAID IN FULL

EFFORT is the fourth cornerstone of our **PERFORMANCE** controls. It's more than working hard. It's the decision to walk directly into discomfort, on purpose, when every part of you wants to stay safe.

The words felt like concrete in my mouth. "I'm sorry man...I'm gonna stay with OSU."

Sitting across from Luke at that restaurant, I watched his face try to hold it together while I walked away from our shared dream. My stomach was in knots. For months, we'd been building Anomaly Sports Group, pouring everything into building this program from scratch. The curriculum took months to develop, and watching student-athletes seeing real sparks, like somebody finally handed them the real playbook for life.

It was purpose. It was potential. And I was walking away from it.

Luke nodded. "I understand, my dude. Family comes first."

Always the professional. Always the brother.

But I knew what this meant.

I was choosing a steady paycheck over the company we built from nothing. Over the work that made my heart beat.

I'd spent seven years in Development at Ohio State. Made a good living. Wore the badge of Buckeye Football. From the outside, it looked like I had it made.

But something was missing.

We created The Complete Athlete Program for that exact reason. No one was preparing student-athletes for what came next, money, identity, relationships, mental health. The stuff that mattered when the cheering stopped.

We built the curriculum ourselves. Raised the money. Walked into Gene Smith's office and got the green light. When we presented it to football and basketball players? Magic. You could see it in their eyes, finally, somebody was giving them the truth.

"We could take this around the country," Luke said after one session. "Every athlete needs this."

He was right. We were on the edge of something powerful. But then came the call from OSU legal. Conflict of interest. Choose: my salaried job with benefits, or the venture we'd been building by hand.

And there I was, choosing safety. Knowing full well I was walking away from what really counted for something.

I couldn't even look him in the eye when I said it. I already knew I was selling out.

"This isn't the end," Luke said, reaching across the table. "We'll find other ways to work together."

I walked out of that restaurant, but a part of me never left the table.

Walking back to my car, I felt hollow. Like I just betrayed the version of me I'd been fighting to become. That steady paycheck suddenly felt like golden handcuffs. I never looked at my OSU job the same way again.

Effort gets praised, but most of the story gets skipped. We've been trained to chase output, stacking hours and knocking out tasks. All surface.

There's the kind of effort that keeps your calendar full, and the kind that changes your life. One looks productive from the outside: meetings, emails, keeping the train moving. The other? It's quieter. It's doing the work you don't want to face. The call that scares you. The conversation you've been avoiding. Stepping toward what matters when every voice in your head says play it safe.

I was clocking 60-hour weeks at OSU. But the one thing I actually needed to do? I kept avoiding it.

Forget whether you're working hard. Ask yourself: **Are you spending that effort on what really counts?**

Or are you climbing a ladder that's leaning against the wrong damn wall?

Luke didn't miss a step after I bailed. He took what we dreamed of and made it real.

And I had to watch it happen without me.

The hardest part? Watching Luke succeed and knowing I should've been right there with him. Not from a place of jealousy. From a place of knowing I turned my back on the harder, better road.

I stayed busy with what I called "work," all the university functions and social events that looked important but didn't actually matter. But deep down, I knew the truth. I chose comfort. And comfort became my burden.

Working hard filled my calendar. Doing the hard work changed my life.

That's when I finally understood what effort really means.

It's doing the scary shit your soul knows you're built for, even when the money and the safety net tell you not to.

Effort looks like sitting across from your best friend and telling the truth you don't want to say. Sometimes it looks like admitting to yourself that you sold out. Sometimes it's waking up the next morning and realizing the mirror's still waiting.

I thought I was choosing security.

I was really choosing regret.

Effort exposes what comfort tries to hide.

This chapter is not about working hard. It's about doing the hard work.

Understanding Effort

I've seen your favorite motivational speakers screaming online, pushing that rise-and-grind, 80-hour workweek hustle as proof of commitment.

And yeah, you're working. But is it the hard work?

The kind that stretches you. The kind that counts. The kind that actually changes something.

Like the other controllables, effort evolves in levels. And the deeper you go, the more it stops being about doing a lot and starts being about doing what matters.

Surface Effort: Busy Ain't Working

This is where the pretenders get caught up in the performance of productivity. The guy at the gym taking selfies between sets. The coworker always saying he's 'slammed', but never getting anything done.

I used to be the king of this space. Early in my fundraising days, I booked back-to-back donor meetings just to feel useful. Morning to night. Full schedule. Felt like I was putting in that work.

But at the end of the day, all I had was a stack of business cards and a bunch of empty promises.

No movement. No momentum. Just motion.

Here's the trap: surface effort feels convincing. The inbox stays full. The hours rack up. The body stays tired. But without direction, none of it adds up to growth.

You've got the look of effort, but not the weight behind it.

Strategic Effort: Hustle Didn't Hit

The breakthrough happens when you stop chasing movement and start choosing impact.

Strategic effort means working with aim. The goal is to "go hard" and to move the needle.

At Ohio State, once I stopped chasing coffee meetings for metrics and started preparing with intention, the numbers followed.

I studied donor profiles, figured out what mattered to them, and connected our mission to it.

And sometimes, one focused conversation did more than a dozen 'coffee chats' ever could.

I saw it all the time, young staff sprinting around trying to look busy, chasing optics. Meanwhile, the veterans were quiet, surgical. Less flash. More results.

Strategic effort means applying force where it counts.

You stop asking, *What should I do next?* And start asking, *What's the most meaningful thing I can do right now?*

Courageous Effort: No Playbook for This

The real courageous effort is the effort that changes you. It's courageous because it's hard to face.

For years, I operated with one foot in. One foot out. A little safety, a little risk. I mixed strategy with security, and called it growth.

But physical effort never scared me. I was afraid of the ownership.

Leaving my comfy job at 50 yrs old? That was courage. Because this time, there was no machine to back me up. No title. No safety net.

Just me.

Building EMP from my kitchen table at 2am. Dialing numbers with a shaky hand. Not as "Raymont from OSU." Just...Raymont. Asking them to bet on me.

I was so nervous that my hands would shake. I was weak because I was finally doing something real. Something that mattered.

That tremor told me I was no longer hiding behind preparation or position. I was exposed. Vulnerable. Alive.

Courageous effort demands giving up comfort more than it requires counting hours. Shedding identity. Letting go of who you've been so you can become who you want to be.

Importance of Effort

Effort shows in what you're building with the energy you spend. Some people grind for years and stay stuck. Others make one hard, courageous move, and everything changes.

Effort has layers. And the deeper you go, the more power you uncover.

Physical Dimension: All Work. No Wins.

Physical effort is easy to spot and easy to misread.

We celebrate hustle. Long hours. I've been that way since growing up in Lorain. I thought pain meant progress and outworking everybody meant I was doing it right.

Yeah, I outworked a lot of people. But I also broke things. My body. My peace. And some relationships I never got back.

From two-a-days in the heat to pushing through pain year-round, I thought effort meant sacrifice at all costs. That if I wasn't hurting, I wasn't doing it right.

In the league, I watched guys destroy themselves in practice...and vanish in three seasons. Their bodies gave out. Their minds went with it. The ones who lasted? They were strategic. They knew when to push and when to pull back. That was a different kind of discipline. One I didn't fully understand until it was too late.

Same story when I worked in Athletics. I ran nonstop. Stacked meetings all day. Late dinners. Felt productive. But results? Mid. I was too drained to show up sharp when it mattered most.

Once I started prepping better and cutting the distractions, protecting my best energy for what mattered became the focus. This redirection elevated everything.

That's physical effort. Not just what you give. What you give up. What you stop wasting. What you stop chasing.

Because exhaustion can trick you into thinking you're doing something noble. But if your effort isn't building something that lasts, all you're doing is burning out.

Mental Dimension: Prep Over Praise

Mental effort is where separation lives. It's not visible. But it's where games get won, before they're played.

In football, it was film study while teammates went out. Running the same plays full-speed for the hundredth time. Because when everything's moving fast, your mind has to move faster.

In fundraising, it looked different, but it was the same grind. People saw the events and the handshakes. What they didn't see was the prep. The hours of research. The way I built donor profiles from scratch, finding the angle that made the mission click.

I was building a strategy. Moving with intention.

Mental effort is making better choices. What matters right now? What creates the biggest impact?

It's the overlooked layer, the one that actually moves things forward.

Emotional Dimension: The Heaviest Lift

This is the level many shy away from: emotional effort.

The calls you don't want to make. The rejection you're scared to risk is what makes your stomach tighten.

I could bench press 300+ pounds, but some days, lifting that phone was heavier than any barbell that I ever lifted. I stared at my phone for 20 minutes just trying to make a cold call. My heart would race and my forehead would sweat a little bit. Because physical and mental effort never exposed me like this did.

The Fisher College of Business was where I remember that feeling well. The work didn't feel significant in my hands, but it did in my mind. Every "no" felt heavier than just a no, it landed as "you're not enough."

Which is exactly why most avoid this kind of work. They'll grind themselves into exhaustion before they'll pick up the phone that asks for something real.

It took me years to understand, on the other side of resistance is where emotional effort lives. Growth shows up there.

Transformation happens in the moments you stop avoiding what makes you feel vulnerable... and do it anyway.

Purposeful Dimension: This One Was Mine

Purposeful effort feeds you while it shapes you. Instead of burning you out, it builds something lasting inside you that grows stronger with every step.

Fundraising was a great job. I was good at it, successful by most measures. But there was always this nagging sense that something was missing.

Then Luke and I created The Complete Athlete Program, and everything took a turn. Teaching student-athletes money, identity, and the communication skills to lead in any space was unique to our program. We researched around the country, and those post-grad skills weren't being taught anywhere. The work felt like alignment with my core, and I was finally doing something that mattered beyond raising money for facilities and just collecting a paycheck.

I could feel it.

The work was demanding, but it didn't drain me like the regular "9 to 5." It energized me. Because purposeful effort doesn't wear you out the same way surface effort does.

Effort never wore me out, but this work refined me.

Even when we spun it into a business with Anomaly Sports, the fire was on full blast. Luke saw it early. It took me a little longer. But once I locked in, I felt what purpose-backed effort really does:

Aligning all your energy toward what actually matters, and more importantly, what matters to you.

Cultivating Effort

Recognizing the different types of effort is just the beginning. When you develop the right kind of effort, your life starts to change. Here's what my journey taught me when it comes to cultivating effort that actually matters:

Aim the Work

The everyday hustler works hard without asking why. They work like hell but don't know where they're going. Burn themselves out chasing whatever gets attention. It sounds noble, but it's not. It's wasteful. Like a car spinning tires, lots of noise and smoke, no forward progress.

I helped raise millions for scholarships and programs that helped our athletes. Development work allowed me to build valuable skills while making meaningful connections. But as time passed,

I felt the growing gap between what I was building and what I was called to build.

The breakthrough came when I asked myself, "Should I be doing this?" and "Am I working on what makes my heart beat?"

When Luke and I first created the Complete Athlete Program, we saw these student-athletes facing challenges that these institutions were not addressing. We had plenty on our plates, but this would be effort toward something that aligned with our deeper purpose. And we had to respond, because the shit mattered.

Chose the Fire

We've been trained to dodge anything that hurts. But effort that changes you comes with pain you choose on purpose. Not pain for the sake of suffering, pain that actually takes you somewhere.

For years, I stayed away from the entrepreneurial leap. Security felt safer. A steady check was easier to stomach than taking a hit. I knew how to handle the problems I already had. What I didn't want was to walk straight into failure trying something new.

The question that changed everything: What discomfort serves my purpose, and what just feeds fear? Calling donors who might reject me, that served a purpose. Staying in a role I'd outgrown just because change was scary, that served fear.

When OSU Legal made me pick between my job and Anomaly, I played it safe. But having to look Luke in the eye and say I was staying? Saying it out loud gutted me. I knew it was the wrong move. I just didn't have the guts to choose the unknown. And I had to live with that.

Built Slow on Purpose

There's a difference between charging every play and building a game that lasts. Between fire and fuel.

I've seen guys crush training camp, then disappear before the season even got rolling. Same thing in the business world, working their asses off then burning out completely. It looks impressive in the moment. But not so much when the breakdown happens.

When we first launched the Complete Athlete Program, I was fired up. It felt purposeful, important, like we were finally doing work that stood for something. But even with all that passion, I had to be smart with my time and energy. I couldn't just power through and expect to sustain it. I had to build in recovery and stay sharp for the moments that moved the mission forward.

Jerome Bettis said it to me early on, I just wasn't ready to hear it. We were at his charity bowling event, and he pulled me aside. Told me I was a good back, but I took too many unnecessary hits. "Run hard when it counts," he said. "But sometimes that last yard ain't worth the collision. Live to run another play."

I heard him, but I didn't really hear him.

Looking back, he was talking about the long game. Running backs who invite contact for no reason? They don't last. Bettis did. Because he knew when to hit and when to step out.

That advice applies to life, not just football. If you're always redlining, never recovering, you won't be around long enough to fulfill the mission. Going hard was easy. Building something I could sustain? That took work.

What good is pride if it breaks you before the job's done?

Overcoming Challenges to Effort

Even when you understand what real effort means, obstacles will test your resolve. Here's what I've learned when everything in you wants to take the easy path, and you push through anyway:

Working Hard vs. Doing the Hard Work

For a long time, I was the busiest underachiever I knew.

It took me years to truly grasp the difference between working hard and doing the hard work. That clarity only hit me after football ended, when the locker room was gone and the quiet got loud.

Early in my Development days, I did what grinders do. I took on every committee, showed up to every event, stayed late for every game. I worked my ass off, on paper. But deep down, I was hiding. My grind was just a disguise for the stuff I was too afraid to face.

The schedule was packed and the boxes were checked. But the hard work? The kind that forces you to look inward and own some shit you've been dodging for years? I avoided that at all costs.

I'd take meetings with anyone...except the donors who pushed me. I'd speak confidently in public...but stay silent in leadership meetings when something didn't sit right. I'd bring up legacy...but kept dodging the conversation that made the difference: whether I was brave enough to leave OSU and go all in with Luke and Anomaly.

Truth is, I was drained from the hours and from the act. I told myself the constant motion meant I was getting somewhere. But I was hiding in the hustle. Staying busy so I wouldn't have to face it, I was helping build someone else's dream because I was too scared to chase mine.

The wild part? Once I stopped ducking the hard stuff and leaned into it, things started to break open. That donor I'd been avoiding? Pushed back, and it turned into my biggest gift. That meeting I almost skipped? I spoke up and walked out with more respect than I ever got staying quiet. And the Anomaly decision, even though I chose wrong, that pain opened something in me that comfort never would've touched.

Working hard fills your calendar. Doing the hard work changes your life.

The real question is: What are you avoiding? Resistance usually points to the door where the work lives.

Gave Too Much

Working in Development at OSU gave me access, influence, and a seat at the table, but that seat came with a cost I didn't see right away.

A normal day might mean chasing down new donors, figuring out what makes each one tick, trying to line up support for the football field, grabbing lunch with a maybe, meeting with the baseball coach to fire up some old players, and ending the day at some happy hour, while still getting ready to help pick the next Development Officer.

And that's just a Tuesday.

At first, it felt like the right thing. Like I was giving back to what built me. I believed in the mission because scholarships changed my life. But little by little, my effort got scattered. I was moving all day, but none of it pointed toward purpose. The work never let up, but my connection to it faded. And the worst part? I didn't even see it happening.

There wasn't time to build the Complete Athlete Program. No space to grow the one thing that actually lit me up. And when new administrators came in trying to "reimagine" what Luke and I had already created? That did it. That was the line, and now I could feel what was broken. It's a rough mirror moment, when you realize you gave up work that meant something for a check and a calendar full of busy.

Overcommitment sneaks up on you. It shows up dressed like responsibility and talks like loyalty. But underneath? It's betrayal and a slow death.

Every time I said yes to another request, I was saying no to something else. And what I was saying no to, over and over, was me. My vision. My purpose..

You don't have to do everything. Learn to say no with intention so you can say yes with direction.

Because purpose won't scream to get your attention. It waits for you to stop running long enough to listen.

Built by the Room

Your environment affects how you show up, and how long you can keep showing up. It either pushes your purpose forward or eats at it little by little, until you're moving nonstop but stuck in the same spot.

I've been in every kind of locker room. Packers. Broncos. Patriots. I had the rare luck, or curse, of arriving right after the parade. Green Bay the year after their Super Bowl. Denver the year after theirs. New England the year right before they took off. I always seemed to show up when the champagne was dry and the egos were loud.

Effort doesn't stand a chance when ego runs the room. You burn more energy managing drama than mastering anything. Guys stop watching film and start watching their backs. Survival takes over. It's talent with no trust, a combination that always stalls out.

But the right culture? It pulls more out of you than you thought you had. In those rare environments where purpose is clear and accountability is real, effort feels different. Cleaner. Sharper. The standard's just the standard, and nobody needs to explain.

Luke wasn't working for OSU, he was just supposed to consult. But the way he gave a damn on a different level. He saw the vision and chased better. No shortcuts. No fluff.

Being around that made me look at my own excuses differently. It exposed where I was coasting, and challenged me to raise my game.

Effort's contagious in both directions. Complacency spreads, but so does conviction.

Struggling to find your drive? Stop blaming your mindset and start checking your surroundings. Look around, what kind of standards are they living by? What do they quietly allow you to get away with?

Your environment is either sharpening your edge, or slowly sanding it down.

Success Story: Kobe Bryant

Before the rings. Before the Mamba mentality. Kobe was 17, fresh out of high school, trying to survive in a league full of grown men. The critics saw an arrogant kid. What they missed was the work.

He was up before the trainers. Getting shots up while teammates slept. After games, win or lose, he'd be in the film room trying to find something he missed. Even on good nights, he walked out carrying mistakes nobody else caught. He couldn't leave them alone.

The obvious stuff, 4 a.m. lifts and thousands of shots, got the attention. But that wasn't what made him different. The average guy leans into his strengths. Kobe went straight at his weaknesses. If something felt off, he went after it. When he couldn't use his right hand, he built up his left. When defenders figured out his footwork, he showed up with something new.

I felt that.

That mindset. That edge that refuses to stay where it's safe. I was doing good work at Ohio State. People respected it. But I knew deep down, I wasn't testing anything. This was safe.

Then came Anomaly. And it was different. No blueprint. No fallback. Just me and Luke, walking into something that could fall apart at any second. Effort showed up there, and it exposed us.

Kobe lived there.

He took shots that could make him the hero, or make him the reason they lost. He held teammates to a bar they didn't ask for. He carried the weight of expectations like it was part of the uniform. Because he refused to cheat his standard.

Then the Achilles injury.

He hit the two free throws and limped off. That was a man finishing the play, because effort doesn't disappear because things went in a direction you weren't expecting.

After basketball, he changed lanes. Built stories and showed up for his daughters. That same fire, just focused somewhere else.

Right before the crash, he was courtside at his daughter's game. Still pushing. Still teaching. The Mamba mentality was being passed on.

Growth is when you stop chasing your own and start creating space for somebody else to chase theirs.

Effort Conclusion: Still Here. Still Working.

Sitting at my desk after fifteen years, I finally faced the truth. I had mastered working hard, but avoided doing the hard work.

I'd built security while my guy built significance with Anomaly.

I chose safety, but purpose kept knocking.

At 51, I finally answered the door. Terrified? Absolutely. But more terrified of waking up one day with a legacy of comfortable regrets that looked good on paper, but didn't feel like mine.

This chapter boils down to one question: Are you working hard...or doing the hard work?

While other players polished what they were already good at, Kobe went straight at the hard work that made him uncomfortable.

I keep replaying that moment, standing there with the development phone in my hand.

How a simple call felt harder than any tackle I'd ever broken. How the most important effort usually happens in the shadows with no feedback, just you deciding.

I used to think effort had to come with noise. Something people could point to and clap for. But the effort that actually changes lives? It happens in silence. In seeds planted so deep they don't bloom until the world forgets you even planted them.

You've got your own versions of that phone call. The ones you keep pushing off. The action isn't what's heavy. It's the honesty it demands before you move.

EMPowered to Act: Step Toward the Work You've Been Avoiding

Spot the Disguise Effort looks impressive when it's loud. Long hours. Constant motion. But is it going anywhere? Scan your work. Where are you working hard to avoid what scares you?

Do the Rep You're Avoiding The hardest part is the action that exposes you. The call. The ask. Name one thing you've delayed because of fear, and move toward it.

Choose What Costs Something The kind of effort that makes things happen won't always come with praise. It'll come with weight. With that pit in your stomach that tells you this step actually means something. Go toward that.

Effort evolves. It grows with you, if you let it.

And that's 100% in your control.

CHAPTER 9

ELITE MINDSET & PERFORMANCE: BUILT FROM EVERY CONTROLLABLE

When people ask me what EMP really means, I think about that afternoon I went back to Lorain.

That decision to finally leave OSU and chase my purpose? That was all eight controllables working together. Belief that I was meant for more. Commitment to stop playing it safe. Adaptability to rebuild my identity. The courage to act on what Tito had been telling me for years.

This is what happens when mindset and performance controls align. They don't just change what you do, they change who you become.

I had just quit my secure job at Ohio State to chase the purpose burning inside me. No salary. No net to catch me if I fell. Just a fire in my gut and a quiet voice hoping I hadn't just made the dumbest decision of my life.

One of the loudest voices pushing me toward that decision belonged to my dude Tito Paul. Back at Ohio State, friendship wasn't even on the table. Like Joey Galloway, Tito and I never really clicked in college. Honestly, I couldn't stand him back then. Fast forward to life after football, and Tito, now a State Farm agent who'd figured out his next chapter while I was still bouncing around unsure, had become one of my closest friends.

I call him "Lil Questions" because the guy never stops asking. By far, he's the nosiest person I know. Whenever he checked in about my job at OSU, I'd give him the safe answer: "Yeah man, it's great. Good job, fun people." But Tito would always cut straight through it: "Ray, you're better than this. You could be doing so much more. You know it. I know it."

And I hated it.

It irritated the hell out of me. It felt like he wasn't supporting me, but he was. It was truth. And I wasn't ready to sit with it.

Instead of hearing it as encouragement, I twisted it. Told myself he was hating. That maybe he was just projecting. That he didn't understand what I had built or how good I really had it. I turned his compliment into a slight. Rewrote his concern as judgment. Anything to keep from having to be honest with myself.

Because the moment I admitted he was right, I had to confront everything I was avoiding.

It's wild how fast your mind will protect your comfort. It'll armor up, block out the truth, and twist up reality to protect the version of you that isn't ready to grow yet. That's what I was doing. Sure, I was coasting, but more than that I was hiding. From my calling. From the fear that I might actually be meant for more and was too afraid to do a damn thing about it.

Tito's words weren't disrespectful. They were a mirror. And mirrors aren't kind when you've been lying to yourself.

That kind of confrontation doesn't feel motivational. It feels like an exposed nerve. But if you're willing to face it, that's where the breakthrough lives. The stuff that makes you flinch? That's usually the stuff that sets you free.

I hadn't booked any keynotes yet. I wasn't fully sure how I'd pay the bills. But I knew I couldn't keep living a safe version of myself. Something had to move.

I grabbed the keys and drove. Back through my old streets, 23rd and East Ave, right next to the junkyard where we used to play. Same potholes and cracked sidewalks. Houses boarded up. Storefronts barely standing. Some parts were worse than I remembered. But that feeling of desperation was the same: get out, or get stuck.

I ended up at George Daniel Field. Lorain High's football team was in the middle of practice.

The shotty grass we used to run on had been replaced with turf. But the energy in the air? Still familiar. Pads popping with that same urgency we used to bring. Coaches yelling. Young dudes grinding, hoping the game might open a door for them.

I sat in the bleachers by myself, just soaking it in.

Same goalposts I used to celebrate under. Same broken skyline. And across town, the old steel mill still stands empty, rusted, and haunting. A reminder of what happens when you never leave and never change.

Honestly? It felt good to be back in my old stomping grounds, but even in that comfort, I had more questions than answers. I was proud. But I was still searching.

Then the head coach spotted me and walked over.

"You're Raymont Harris, right? You mind saying a few words to the team?"

My stomach dropped. I didn't have anything prepared. No notes to lean on. Just me and the same butterflies I had the last time I was in this stadium.

Damn...I'm not ready for this. What the hell do I even say?

I'd just quit my job at OSU to be a speaker. This is what I said I wanted.

I nodded. I couldn't say no. Not here. Not to my school. Not to these kids.

But truthfully? I wasn't standing there full of confidence. I was standing there hoping I didn't blow the opportunity I'd just left everything to chase.

Next thing I know, I'm standing in front of forty kids. Sweaty pads. Tired eyes. Looking up at me like maybe I had something worth hearing.

Looking at them was like looking at ghosts of my younger self. These kids walked past my old jersey in the locker room every day. Most probably didn't know who I was or what I had to survive just to get out.

"That's my NFL jersey you guys walk past every day," I told them. "And here are the facts... I was third string my junior year. I only started seven games my entire high school career."

Something in the air shifted with the guys. Not because I'd played in the league.-But because they realized that whatever that burn was inside them...I had it too.

After the talk, most of them went back to practice.

Except one.

Skinny kid. All elbows and raw confidence. He came right up to me. No hesitation.

"I'm not starting yet, but I will be soon," he said. "No cap...you'll be hearing my name, Mr. Harris."

He didn't say it like a wish.

He said it like a promise.

That kid right there, that's who EMP is for.

The ones who haven't been crowned but still believe there's a path to the throne.

That conversation confirmed it.

I left the safety net behind. And for the first time in years, I actually felt free.

EMP ain't a workbook. It's a mindset. A lifestyle. A way to stand up when shit gets heavy.

It means showing up when doubt's louder than direction.

Working like the spotlight's already on you, even when the world doesn't know your name.

It's trusting the work long before it ever pays you back.

EMP gave me something solid to hold when everything else fell apart.

The truth is quiet. No fanfare. No applause. EMP is the truth.

And that truth carried me through the storm.

Now it's mine to hand over.

The Birth of Control the Controllables

People always ask me the same thing: "How the hell did you make it out of Lorain and get to where you are now?"

For years, I didn't have a real answer. I'd throw out the usual 'work hard', 'stay positive', 'never quit'. Words people repeat because they can't admit they don't know what really works. But the question kept coming. Sometimes casual. Sometimes from people who *really* wanted to know.

I forced myself to sit with it.

No camera. No crowd. Just me, running through every moment that nearly broke me and the ones that couldn't.

What actually got me through? It wasn't magic. It wasn't luck. It was a handful of things I learned how to control.

I started noticing a pattern: same tools, same mindset. It kept showing up when the pressure hit, whether I was on the way up or clawing back from nothing.

These were the tools that held me together when everything else was falling apart.

I leaned on them when football ended and I had no idea who I was. I leaned on them during those four ugly years in mortgages when I was just trying to stay alive. I leaned on them through fifteen years at Ohio State while I was learning how to fundraise and keep evolving. And I leaned on them again when I finally walked away from all that security to chase something I couldn't explain but knew was my purpose.

These tools helped me climb. And when I crashed? They helped me rebuild.

I realized this system works for anyone, no matter where you are stuck, falling, lost, or starting over.

The power's already in your hands. It's just time to use it on purpose.

Control the Controllables was born right there. It came from moments that gutted me. From bleeding while still trying to climb. Trying to figure out who I really was and what would carry me forward when nothing else would.

MINDSET and PERFORMANCE: The Complete System

As I refined this system, I realized these eight controllables naturally break down into two main groups:

MINDSET Controls (B.P.C.P.):

- **BELIEF:** Your foundation that something better is possible
- **POSITIVITY:** Your ability to spot opportunities when everyone else sees problems
- **COMMITMENT:** Your dedication to keep going when it's no longer convenient
- **PATIENCE:** Your understanding of how time and process actually work

PERFORMANCE Controls (C.A.R.E.):

- **CONSISTENCY:** Your ability to show up and deliver, regardless of how you feel
- **ADAPTABILITY:** Your skill at adjusting when life changes (and it always changes)
- **RESILIENCE:** Your power to bounce back stronger after getting knocked down
- **EFFORT:** Your energy focused on stuff that actually matters

This framework was built for the stage. The principles came from real life. It's how people survive 'harder' and come out stronger.

A lot of motivation out there tells you to just push through and stay positive. Cool. But it's not enough. Not when life gets crazy. Not when your mind's breaking down and nobody sees it.

What makes EMP different is it lives in both the performance world and the mindset world. It lives where the two worlds collide where your thoughts and actions either hold you up or drag you under.

I've seen what folks carry. Depression. Addiction. Trauma. Childhood shit that still haunts them. Stuff that never makes it to the résumé. And here's the truth: none of the other controllables mean a thing if your mental health is falling apart.

The mindset side of EMP helps you steady your head when everything's pulling at you. Keeps you from folding when the pressure's high and the path ain't clear.

The performance side? It gets you through the mess. How you keep showing up when your body's tired and your confidence is leaking. How you get it done without losing yourself in the process.

EMP makes space for the whole person. Space for the part of you chasing goals meeting the tired part, the part carrying old wounds, the part unsure if any of this will work. Not just who you want to become, but who you are right now. This system pushes your dreams and respects the scars.

The Integrated System: How MINDSET and PERFORMANCE Work Together

Mindset and Performance feed off each other. One fuels the fire, the other keeps it burning. The mindset controls activate the performance controls. The performance controls reinforce the mindset controls. Together, they create something greater than either could produce alone.

Let me show you how this integration works:

BELIEF Starts It All

Every journey begins here with belief that transcends your current reality. Belief is what keeps the other controllables alive. Without it, the rest get shaky real fast. It's the foundation everything else stands on.

When I stepped onto Ohio State's campus as a freshman, my belief wasn't all the way there. I believed I belonged but I still questioned if I was good enough, if I'd ever get real minutes.

That kind of doubt stalls a lot of guys. Keeps them half-stepping or walking away. But the belief I built in Lorain that wired me for moments like that. The words from Mr. Herrmann or those battles where I had to prove I belonged gave me just enough to keep going.

Belief got built the only way it ever does. It grew with every decision I made to keep going. The more I committed, the more it grew. The more I prepared, the more solid it got. All the controllables started backing each other up like a loop that got stronger every time I kept showing up.

It works like this: you do the work, your belief grows. You believe more, so you do more. And over time, that loop becomes who you are.

The Mental Health Connection: How PERFORMANCE Controls Wellbeing

Most of the stuff out there just tells you to push harder. Like willpower's supposed to fix everything. But that ain't real life.

What I had to rewire I used to think effort was always the issue, but it's not. Some people are just trying not to break. Survival takes everything they've got. Not everybody's dragging their feet some are dragging their pain.

Performance controls come in right there they give you something solid to lean on when nothing else makes sense. When the world feels like it's caving in, these are the things that keep you from going with it.

CONSISTENCY gives your mind something solid when everything else feels like it's falling apart. Depression makes every move feel heavy, but consistency breaks it down. Just do the next thing. Simple as that. Anxiety floods your head with too many options. But a simple routine? That gives you direction. Your emotions might swing wild, but that steady rhythm becomes your grip when the storm hits hardest.

ADAPTABILITY shuts down that perfectionist lie the one that says if it ain't perfect, it's a failure. Just me, running through every moment that nearly broke me and the ones that couldn't. It throws curveballs. Being able to pivot without losing yourself is what keeps you moving. Adaptability gives you choices. And when the pressure is high, choices keep you sane.

RESILIENCE is building while it still hurts. Life doesn't pause. You stand up bleeding and keep finding meaning in the work. The things that tried to break you? They end up building you. The wounds turn into protection. Those scars? That's your armor.

EFFORT is where the grind goes. You can push all day and feel empty if you're aiming at the wrong thing. But when it's locked on to purpose? That work fills you up. It steadies you. The chaos fades. You stop running in circles and start building something that holds. This is the line between burning out and breaking through.

When football ended, I wasn't okay. And no amount of positive thinking was gonna fix that. That first Monday after clearing out my locker, I woke up with no routine... and no identity. It hit me lying there at 3AM, staring at the ceiling, thinking Who the hell am I now?

That elite athlete mindset runs deep. It's in your bones. When that part of you dies, rebuilding from nothing demands everything. The mental fight starts there.

I leaned on what I had left. Consistency gave me a rhythm to hold. Adaptability helped me see new ways forward. Resilience kept me moving when I wanted to disappear. Effort gave the pain somewhere to go.

That's EMP. Not a bunch of slogans. It's a system that works when nothing else does. When it's just you... and everything feels heavy as hell.

Implementing the Complete EMP System in Your Life

Build Daily Practices for Both MINDSET and PERFORMANCE

There's a big difference between knowing this work and living it. You can understand every controllable in theory and still crumble when life gets heavy. This part is where it gets real day by day, moment by moment. Building habits that hold when the struggle gets real.

MINDSET Practices:

BELIEF Practice

Start your day by getting clear on what you're building toward. I'm not talking about some random 'vision board' dream I mean something you can actually see. The details. How it shows up in your world. This kind of focus rewires your brain over time. It makes the work feel less random. It reminds you that your direction is on point.

POSITIVITY Practice

Catch the spiral early. When your mind starts racing with "this won't work," stop and call it out. Then hit it with receipts. Remind yourself what you've already come through. This is just reminding your brain what it already knows. It sharpens your edge and keeps you steady when the negativity starts creeping in.

COMMITMENT Practice

Ask yourself one thing: Do your actions line up with what you say matters? Not in theory. Not next week. Today. Your habits and energy show what you're really committed to. If the gap's too wide, close it. Make at least one move today that proves your word means something.

PATIENCE Practice

When things feel stuck, zoom out. Don't get lost staring at the wall in front of you. Look back at where you started. Then get clear on the next move that matters just one. You don't have to love the pace. You just need to keep walking. Patience builds when you stop obsessing over when it's happening and start owning how you're showing up while it unfolds.

PERFORMANCE Practices:

CONSISTENCY Practice

Motivation comes and goes. Build a setup that doesn't care how you feel. Use triggers you can see. Feedback you can track. People who'll check you without flinching. Let your environment carry some weight so you're not out here trying to muscle through every day alone.

ADAPTABILITY Practice

Don't wait for chaos to teach you the lesson. Try new approaches now before you're forced to. Test tools. Try things that make you uncomfortable. Speak up in spaces where you're not the expert. Stretch your range on purpose, so when the unexpected shows up, you're already built for it.

RESILIENCE Practice

What actually gets you back up when things fall apart? Lock that in. Could be a process. Could be a person. Might be movement. Might be quiet. But you need to know it before the breakdown not after. The hits are coming. Your bounce-back plan better be ready.

EFFORT Practice

Pick a window each day and make it yours. Block it off. Fire zone only no emails, no distractions, no busy work. Just the one thing that actually moves your life. Protect it like it pays your bills. Because at some point, it will.

You won't master this overnight. Some days you'll overthink. Other days you'll blow it completely. It's all part of it. What matters is staying in it. Keep showing up. Keep adjusting. Bit by bit, it starts to hold. Starts to mean something. Starts to feel solid.

The EMP Promise: You've Got Everything You Need

I've watched this system work in every kind of space. Athletes trying to find their way. Leaders rebuilding after the fall. Folks making risky moves with no net. People healing from stuff that would break most of us. Teams chasing more than just stats and spotlight.

Where they started never decided the outcome. What changed was simple: they quit waiting around. Started moving. Built something that felt like theirs.

Life stayed hard. But the fog cleared. And the hits? They still came. But now they fed the fire. You move with intention. You know what matters and your steps match it.

When these controllables start working together, your life seriously changes. Straight up.

When It All Starts Hitting the Same Target

A lot of folks are grinding all day and going nowhere. Hustling with no real aim. Worn out by Friday, nothing to show for it. Doing ten things at once, stuck in the same damn spot.

EMP lines your stuff up. Belief points the way. Commitment keeps you from drifting. Consistency builds the rhythm. And when all of it's in place? Your effort lands with force.

That scattered energy you used to bleed out everywhere? It starts working like a weapon. Tight. Focused. The busy work falls off. You stop sprinting in circles and start moving with purpose. Just know when your effort lines up with what matters, it changes the game. The regular hustle starts making dents.

From Defense to Offense

Too many people live life on defense. Just reacting. Bouncing from one fire to the next. Answering emails, fixing messes, dealing with other people's timelines. Living inside somebody else's playbook.

EMP flips that. Gives you the ball.

Belief lets you see something that ain't here yet. Commitment locks you into building it. Adaptability lets you pivot without losing your aim. Resilience keeps you swinging when the hits don't stop.

Life still comes at you. But now you're moving with it writing the next chapter while the last one's still on fire.

Your EMP Legacy

The *Control the Controllables* framework functions as a system, like Voltron or the Wu-Tang Clan. Every controllable has value by itself. But when they start overlapping when belief fuels effort, when resilience leans on consistency the system starts moving like a machine.

Just like Voltron's lions that combine to form one powerful robot, or Wu-Tang's nine MCs who each brought different skills to create something legendary, each element in the CTC framework Belief, Positivity, Commitment, Patience, Consistency, Adaptability, Resilience, and Effort serves a unique role. Alone, they're strong. But together? They're a force.

A lot of folks bank on mindset alone just belief, positivity, commitment. Going in without the full system? It's like rolling into battle with half of Voltron.

The real power comes when mindset and performance controls connect. This is what makes EMP different. It gives you both the motivation and the ability to execute under pressure, adapting when things twist, and staying resilient when life throws punches.

Master one, and you improve.

Master them all, and you're damn near unstoppable.

Think back on every story we've covered. From those cold Lorain mornings to NFL fields. From bank branch offices to speaking stages. From comfortable salaries to betting on yourself. The choice to keep growing made all the difference, pushing forward and believing even when everything around you was screaming to stop.

After speaking to a Power 5 team, a freshman pulls me aside. He's frustrated no playing time, thinking about hitting the transfer portal. He swears he's working, but it's not happening fast enough.

"What's in your control right now?" I ask him.

He starts listing external things coaches, depth charts, competition.

"No," I tell him. "What's REALLY in your control?"

We break it down: Commitment. Consistency. Effort. Adaptability. We check in periodically, and two months later, he texts me: "Coach just told me I've earned a spot in the rotation. Real talk...Appreciate you OG!"

He didn't transfer. He controlled what he could, and the rest took care of itself.

The legacy of EMP is this: build it in yourself so you can build it in others. What you've lived through becomes the reason someone else makes it.

Control isn't given. It's claimed. Your move.

Before you put this into action, there's something I haven't said yet, something you deserve to know.

EMP Was Born from My Mistakes

EMP was born in chaos, long before clarity ever showed its face. Missed calls. Missed chances. Public wins with private messes. Me chasing control in places that never had it.

When I started Elite Mindset & Performance, I didn't have a playbook. I had belief in the message and a name that might get me in the room. But name recognition doesn't build systems. It doesn't fix sloppy processes. It doesn't help when the phone stops ringing. I had to lead before anything was built. And I had to get real honest about what wasn't working.

I overpromised a lot. I didn't know how to scale. And some days I wondered if I even had the right to teach any of this. How could I preach consistency while scrambling to stay consistent behind the scenes? How could I talk about belief when mine kept getting punched in the mouth?

I didn't quit. But I had to admit something I didn't want to say out loud. I understood the message before I ever lived it at this level.

That's why this book exists. To hand you the system I had to build the hard way. The same one I wish I had when everything was breaking around me. Forget brand-building. Forget the polished stories.

EMP is for the ones who know how to perform, but still feel stuck. For the leaders who show up strong, then question everything when it's quiet. For the version of me that needed something solid to stand on, not just something inspiring to hear.

Everything changed when I stopped trying to protect the image and started building the foundation.

CHAPTER 10

THE COMBO MANUAL: MAKING EMP WORK IN REAL LIFE

Before You Start: Your First 30 Days With EMP

This might feel exciting right now. You've got this new language. Clarity. Momentum. But here's what's coming:

You'll try to apply this, and life won't care. Old habits will fight back. You'll start noticing how inconsistent your circle really is. You'll question whether you're built for it. And maybe the hardest part: you'll see the gap between who you are and who you thought you were.

That's normal. That's Day One. You're not broken. You're just finally aware. And once you see it, you can't unsee it. That's where power starts.

This system doesn't work because it feels good. It works because it's grounded. Expect friction. Expect resistance. But if you stay with it for 10 days, 20 days, 30 days, you'll feel something you haven't felt in a long time. Control.

Turn the page when you're ready to stop reacting and start responding.

Making EMP Work in Real Life

By now, you've seen what each controllable can do. You've read the stories. You've felt the moments. But life doesn't come at you one skill at a time. It throws everything at once: chaos, curveballs, silence, pressure, expectation. This chapter is about giving you a system to respond.

Not a checklist. A toolbox. Not motivation. A game plan.

When you know how to combine the eight controls, you stop reacting to life and start responding with power.

These are your EMP combos. Use them. Remix them. Come back to them when you're stuck. They're built for the real world, not just the book.

The System in Action: Powerful Controllable Combinations

While all eight controllables work together, certain combinations create especially powerful synergy, particular pairings that address specific challenges with unmatched effectiveness. Understanding these strategic combinations allows you to activate the right tools at the right time.

BELIEF × COMMITMENT: Sustainable Direction

This intersection made my transition into fullback possible. If I'd just committed to the position change without believing I could excel there, I would have given decent effort without the passion that creates excellence. If I'd just talked a big game about being great without putting in the work on blocking schemes and new responsibilities, I'd have wasted that opportunity. The combination gave me both direction and drive. I wasn't just doing a job, I was becoming something I believed in.

ADAPTABILITY × CONSISTENCY: Dynamic Stability

This combo powered all my career changes. Going from player to broadcaster to development to entrepreneur meant learning completely different games. New skills. New mindsets. New ways to measure success. But through all that, my standards never changed: the preparation, the keeping it real, the commitment to making a difference. This mix keeps you relevant no matter what happens. You don't get left behind because you can adapt. You don't get lost because your core values give you direction.

POSITIVITY × RESILIENCE: Sustainable Recovery

When my NFL career crashed to an end, I needed both Positivity and Resilience desperately. That transition broke parts of me I didn't even know could break. I sat in my basement watching games I should've been playing in. Dodged questions about "what's next." That hollow ache deep in my bones when someone introduced me as "former NFL player Raymont Harris." It hit hard. But the mindset I'd built wouldn't let me stay broken. I felt the pain but still believed in what could be next. I faced the loss but focused on what I still had. I honored the end of that chapter while starting to write the next one.

Now that you've seen how the right controllables can work together in real life, here's a guide for when to use them in yours.

Your EMP Combos: Real-Life Playbook

WHEN YOU FEEL STUCK IN NEUTRAL

Belief + Adaptability + Patience

You don't need more hype. You need direction. Belief gets you back in motion. Adaptability keeps you from forcing old strategies that no longer work. Patience makes sure you don't bail before traction hits. This combo is for when you're putting in work but nothing's moving, when effort isn't the issue, clarity is.

WHEN YOU'RE STARTING OVER

Belief + Commitment + Resilience

Whether you're recovering from a setback, stepping into a new chapter, or rebuilding your identity, this trio is your foundation. Belief reminds you you're not done. Commitment locks in your focus. Resilience lets you bounce when it gets rough. You're not starting from scratch, you're starting from experience.

WHEN YOU NEED TO LEVEL UP

Effort + Consistency + Commitment

This one's about getting sharper. No fluff. No shortcuts. Effort brings the heat. Consistency gives it structure. Commitment keeps the edge when nobody's pushing you but you.

WHEN LIFE GETS LOUD

Resilience + Patience + Adaptability

When everything's spinning, this combo keeps you grounded. Resilience helps you breathe through the chaos. Patience keeps your decisions clear. Adaptability makes sure you don't freeze when the world turns.

WHEN DOUBT CREEPS IN

Belief + Positivity + Commitment

Your confidence is leaking. The voice in your head is getting louder. This trio plugs that leak. Belief reminds you who the hell you are. Positivity keeps your lens clear. Commitment makes sure you don't slow down just because your mind is playing games.

WHEN RESULTS AREN'T COMING

Effort + Patience + Consistency

Perfect for the plateau. When you're doing the work, but the outcome isn't matching the grind. Effort keeps the fire lit. Patience keeps you from forcing results. Consistency locks in the habits that eventually break through.

WHEN EVERYTHING CHANGES AT ONCE

Adaptability + Resilience + Belief

New team. New job. New city. Or maybe you just lost something you thought was forever. Adaptability lets you flow. Resilience makes sure you don't snap. Belief gives you the anchor. This combo is for those "damn, this is real" seasons.

WHEN YOU FEEL INVISIBLE

Commitment + Resilience + Positivity

You're showing up, but no one's clapping. You're working, but nobody's watching. This one's for staying strong when recognition lags behind reality. Commitment keeps you showing up. Resilience keeps you from cracking. Positivity helps you see the small wins until the world catches up.

WHEN YOU'RE OVERTHINKING

Consistency + Commitment + Belief

Analysis paralysis. Every option looks right and wrong. Consistency quiets the noise with routine. Commitment gets you moving. Belief keeps you locked in.

WHEN YOU'RE LEADING OTHERS

Positivity + Effort + Adaptability

You set the tone. That means how you show up matters. This combo helps you lead without needing a title. Positivity lights the path. Effort earns respect. Adaptability helps you guide others through uncertainty. Be who you needed when you were struggling.

WHEN YOU'RE GROWING FASTER THAN YOUR CIRCUMSTANCES

Belief + Patience + Adaptability

You've outgrown your role, your team, maybe even your environment. But the opportunity hasn't caught up yet. Don't shrink. Don't rush. Believe in what's next, adapt to what you can control, and stay patient until the door opens.

WHEN IT'S TIME TO REINVENT YOURSELF

Adaptability + Belief + Effort + Resilience

You're not pivoting. You're evolving. Adaptability opens the door. Belief gives you permission. Effort puts action behind intention. Resilience lets you build the new version under pressure.

WHEN YOU'RE WAITING TOO LONG TO BE READY

Belief + Adaptability + Effort

You're stuck in prep mode: researching, planning, analyzing. This combo is about movement. Belief reminds you that you're ready enough. Effort turns thoughts into action. Adaptability lets you adjust on the fly.

WHEN YOU'RE DEALING WITH DOUBTERS

Commitment + Consistency + Positivity

You don't need to convince anybody. Just stay at it. Commitment locks you in. Consistency makes your work speak for itself. Positivity keeps you from absorbing their doubt as your own.

WHEN YOU'RE PUSHING THROUGH PAIN

Resilience + Effort + Patience

Physical pain. Emotional pain. The kind that wears you down slow. This combo helps you manage the load. Resilience gets you through the rough spots. Effort gives it somewhere to go. Patience reminds you it won't hurt like this forever.

WHEN YOU'RE BUILDING SOMETHING NEW

Belief + Effort + Consistency

The early stages are quiet. Nobody sees the work but you. Belief keeps you showing up. Effort sets the tone. Consistency turns day one into day one hundred.

WHEN YOU'RE COMING BACK FROM FAILURE

Resilience + Commitment + Belief

You took a hit. This combo is for the rebuild. Resilience lets you learn without folding. Commitment gets you back in it. Belief makes sure you don't drag shame into your next chapter.

WHEN YOU'RE FACING PRESSURE MOMENTS

Positivity + Adaptability + Effort

The spotlight's on. Stakes are high. This combo helps you stay loose. Positivity keeps the fear small. Adaptability keeps you fluid. Effort makes sure you leave it all out there.

WHEN YOU NEED TO REFOCUS

Consistency + Belief + Effort

You've been distracted. This combo locks you back in. Consistency rebuilds your rhythm. Belief gives your energy a target. Effort gets you moving.

WHEN YOU'RE IN A DRY SEASON

Positivity + Resilience + Commitment

You're showing up and not much is changing. This combo helps you stay the course. Patience calms the panic. Resilience holds the line. Commitment reminds you why you started.

Final Word

These combos are tools for real life. When life tests you, EMP gives you the controls you need. Pull them when it counts. Keep becoming who you said you'd be.

What happens next is always 100% in your control.

SPECIAL ACKNOWLEDGMENTS

This book didn't come out of nowhere. I didn't build it alone.

To Tracie - Your partnership, love, and leadership fuel everything I do. You are the foundation EMP stands on today and the reason this vision continues to grow.

To Nicole - In the beginning, *Control the Controllables* was just scattered thoughts. You helped me put language around the framework and gave structure to the mindset and performance controls. You laid the first bricks on which I built.

To my family and my closest circle - Thank you for holding me up through every season.

And to every team, company, and person who sat in the crowd and gave me their attention - You gave me the push to keep refining this message until it could live on these pages.

This isn't just a book. It's a manual for pressure. If you're reading it, it's in your hands now.